Who's in Charge?

The Mixed Ownership Corporation in Canada

Who's in Charge?

The Mixed Ownership Corporation in Canada

by

Stephen Brooks

The Institute for Research on Public Policy
L'Institut de recherches politiques

Printed in Canada

Legal Deposit Second Quarter
Bibliothèque nationale du Québec

Canadian Cataloguing in Publication Data

Brooks, Stephen, 1956-
Who's in charge? : the mixed ownership corporation in Canada

Foreword and summary in English and French
ISBN 0-88645-051-9

1. Government ownerships--Canada. 2. Corporations, Government--Canada. 3. Industry and state--Canada. I. Institute for Research on Public Policy. II. Title.

HD4005.B76 1987 338.6'2'0971 C87-090132-X

The camera-ready copy for this publication was created on a Xerox 6085 Desktop Publishing System.

The Institute for Research on Public Policy/
L'Institut de recherches politiques
P.O. Box 3670 South
Halifax, Nova Scotia B3J 3K6

Contents

Foreword

In a February 7, 1987 *Globe and Mail* column entitled "The Air Canada Loop", Jeffrey Simpson observes that "a piecemeal privatization with the government retaining a minority shareholding may be the only way to reconcile reality with the Mulroney pronouncement (that Air Canada is not for sale)". He goes on to argue that "however politically satisfying that solution might be, it would make no economic or public policy sense". It is precisely this issue – the merits of the mixed ownership corporation as a vehicle of public policy – which Professor Brooks tackles in this book. On the strength of his careful documentation and analysis of three distinct types of mixed ownership arrangement, Professor Brooks charts the hidden dangers which await a provincial or federal government attempting to attain a public policy goal by entering into a joint ownership arrangement with private capital. Professor Brooks' counsel is one of caution: while mixed ownership corporations may not be inherently unworkable, the record suggests that corporate managers and private shareholders have sufficient tools at hand to frustrate the policy intentions of public shareholders. As Professor Brooks puts it: "The central argument of this study is that the mixed ownership corporation involves an ambiguous form of organization which limits the ability of the government shareholder to impose its policy goals on that organization when these seriously conflict with those of management and/or private sector shareholders".

Investigation of the viability of institutions such as mixed ownership corporations is exactly what the Institute's Governability Research Program is designed to undertake. It is the Institute's view that the institutions and processes that we as a nation employ to initiate, make and deliver public policy are often vital determinants of the shape of the agenda we set, the policies we adopt, the success of these policies and our perceptions as citizens of the effectiveness and legitimacy of government itself. This research program reflects a continuing commitment by IRPP to the examination of key problems in the representative and executive institutions of governance in Canada.

The need for such a continuing research effort is obvious. Except for occasional commendable assaults by royal commissions, government task forces or research councils, and individuals in the academic community, on problems relating to specific aspects of the "machinery of government", this country has in the past mounted little sustained effort to monitor our processes of governance and to examine and debate potential reforms to public institutions. This gap in our policy research net has encouraged a generally low level of debate about the adaptability and reform of our structures and institutions of government.

Nowhere has this problem been more evident than in the growing controversy surrounding government's intervention as an owner in the corporate economy. Questions about the rationale for Crown ownership of corporations, the efficiency and effectiveness of government held companies and their accountability to government and Parliament have too often been met with replies driven by rhetoric, inadequate theoretical models or hunches based on little or no empirical data. In previous Institute volumes – most notably Doern and Tupper, *Crown Corporations and Public Policy in Canada*, and Kierans and Stanbury, *Papers on Privatization* – the Institute has tried to dig a little deeper into the arguments surrounding the viability and utility of public ownership. In this study Professor Brooks probes even further into difficult terrain on the frontier between the public and private sector. His findings raise serious concerns about the viability of the mixed ownership corporation as a vehicle of public policy.

This book is one of several projects in the Institute's Governability Research Program which is made possible by a grant from the Max Bell Business-Government Studies Program. I particularly want to thank Professor Jim Gillies, of York University, for his role in support of this research.

Rod Dobell
President

March 1987

Avant-propos

Dans un article du *Globe and Mail* du 7 février 1987, intitulé "The Air Canada Loop" (Le looping d'Air Canada), Jeffrey Simpson fait observer qu'une privatisation fragmentaire, permettant au gouvernement de retenir un paquet d'actions minoritaires, est sans doute le seul moyen de concilier la réalité avec la déclaration de Mulroney que "Air Canada n'est pas à vendre". Le journaliste continue en disant que, "quels que soient les avantages sociaux de cette solution, celle-ci, d'un point de vue économique ou de politique générale, ne fait aucun sens." C'est précisément à cette question des mérites de la corporation en propriété mixte, considérée comme instrument de politique générale, que le professeur Brooks s'affronte dans ce livre. A partir d'une documentation et d'une analyse soigneuses de trois catégories distinctes d'associations en propriété mixte, le professeur Brooks dresse un état des dangers auxquels s'exposerait un gouvernement provincial ou fédéral qui essaierait de parvenir à un objectif de politique générale en s'associant en participation avec le capital privé. Le professeur Brooks conseille la prudence; sans doute le fonctionnement d'une corporation mixte n'est pas une impossibilité en soi, mais l'expérience montre que les dirigeants de la corporation et les actionnaires privés ont assez de moyens en leur pouvoir pour neutraliser le projet de politique générale du propriétaire public. Comme l'indique l'auteur, "l'argument majeur de cette étude réside dans le fait que la corporation en propriété mixte est d'un type ambigu qui restreint la liberté d'action du partenaire public, quand il s'agit pour lui d'imposer ses vues de politique générale, si celles-ci sont en contradiction avec les propres objectifs de la direction et/ou des actionnaires privés."

La recherche sur la viabilité du genre des corporations mixtes entre exactement dans le cadre des activités du programme de recherche de l'Institut sur la capacité de gouverner. L'Institut est persuadé que les institutions et procédures adoptées pour amorcer, créer et mettre en pratique une politique générale sont souvent des déterminants décisifs de la physionomie du programme d'action que nous établissons, des politiques que nous adoptons, du succès de ces politiques et de notre perception, comme citoyens, de l'efficacité et de la légitimité du gouvernement lui-même. Ce programme de recherche est le reflet de l'engagement pris par l'IRP d'examiner les problèmes-clé qui se posent dans les institutions représentatives et exécutives gouvernementales au Canada.

Le besoin d'un effort de recherche continu dans ce domaine est évident. A l'exception d'occasionnelles et de louables tentatives effectuées par des commissions royales, des comités d'enquête, des conseils de recherche gouvernementaux, des universitaires, pour étudier tel ou tel aspect spécifique des rouages gouvernementaux, on trouve, dans le passé, peu d'efforts soutenus pour contrôler la bonne exécution de nos pratiques gouvernementales ou pour étudier et discuter d'eventuelles réformes des institutions publiques. Cette lacune dans notre réseau de recherche en matière politique a eu pour conséquence un niveau de discussion généralement faible, relativement aux facultés d'adaptation et de réforme de nos structures et institutions de gouvernement.

Le problème n'est apparu nulle part aussi évident que dans la controverse grandissante sur le rôle de l'Etat, comme propriétaire de compagnies. Les questions au sujet des raisons derrière la possession de corporations par la Couronne, de l'efficacité et des effets des compagnies appartenant au gouvernement, de la responsabilité de celles-ci devant le gouvernement et le Parlement ont trop souvent été réglées par des réponses rhétoriques, par la présentation de modèles théoriques inadéquats, ou encore par des intuitions reposant sur des faits empiriques rares ou sans existence. Dans des volumes antérieurs – plus particulièrement *Crown Corporations and Public Policy in Canada*, de Doern et Tupper, et *Papers Privatization*, de Kierans et Stanbury – l'Institut avait commencé à examiner les arguments touchant à la viabilité et à l'utilité de la propriété publique. Dans cette étude, le professeur Brooks pousse plus avant l'enquête et s'engage sur un terrain difficile, à la frontière entre le public et le privé. Ce qu'il découvre suscite de sérieuses inquiétudes quant à la pertinence du rôle de la corporation en propriété mixte comme instrument de politique générale.

Ce livre représente un projet parmi d'autres entrepris dans le cadre du programme de recherche de l'Institut portant sur la capacité de gouverner. Il a été rendu possible par une subvention du Max Bell Business-Government Studies Program. Je tiens à remercier particulièrement le professeur Jim Gillies, de l'Université York, pour l'appui qu'il a apporté à cette recherche.

Rod Dobell
Président

Mars 1987

Acknowledgements

A number of debts were incurred during the research and writing of this study, and it is my pleasure to acknowledge them. I should like to thank Maureen Appel Molot and Jean Kirk Laux for their thoughtful comments and advice from the very beginning of this project to its completion. I should also like to thank Allan Tupper, Bruce Doern, Kent Weaver and Michael Whittington for their comments on various incarnations of the present work. A great debt is owed to the IRPP's Research Director, John Langford, whose critical eye helped to remove some of the rough edges from the analysis.

I am grateful to the University of Windsor for secretarial and financial support. Particular mention must be made of Mrs. Barbara Faria, of the Political Science Department, and the staff of the Word Processing Centre.

Finally, I should like to thank Christine Brooks for her encouragement and forbearance during the writing of this book.

The Author

Stephen Brooks has taught in the Department of Politics at Brock University, and currently teaches in the areas of Canadian politics and public policy at the University of Windsor. He has published a number of articles on state investment in Canada and Western Europe, along with *Political Thought in Canada: Contemporary Perspectives* (editor) and *Between Clerisy and Vanguard: Social Scientists and Politics in Canada* (co-authored with Alain G. Gagnon: forthcoming).

Executive Summary

This study examines the opportunities and limitations of the mixed ownership corporation (MOC), in which ownership is divided between the state and private investors, as a policy instrument. Previous studies of the MOC have identified the rights of private shareholders as the main obstacle to government influence on the behaviour of such a corporation. Based on an analysis of several cases where the state shareholder's goals for the MOC conflicted with those of the corporation's managers, it appears that a government's ability to pursue non-commercial goals through the MOC is highly situational, depending on the precise form of the state's relationship to the MOC and the reaction of interests not directly associated with the corporation to government influence attempts.

The Canada Development Corporation, Telesat Canada and shareholdings of the Caisse de dépôt et placement du Québec are the MOCs examined in this study. Personal interviews with corporate and state officials provided much of the data for the analysis of conflicting goals for the MOC, and how these differences were resolved.

After establishing the general limitations of the MOC as a policy instrument, the particular differences between the cases in the social returns on the public's invested capital are considered. These vary from the relative success of Telesat in promoting the growth of a domestic manufacturing capacity in satellites, through the supportive relationship of some of the Caisse shareholdings to Quebec's economic development, to the nebulous social returns that the Canadian public received from its investment in the CDC.

Abrégé

Cette étude examine les avantages et inconvénients de la corporation en propriété mixte (CPM), dans laquelle, pour des raisons pratiques, le droit de propriété est divisé entre l'Etat et des investisseurs privés. Des études antérieures sur les CPM ont montré que les droits des actionnaires privés constituaient l'obstacle principal à l'influence du gouvernement dans la conduite d'une telle corporation. D'après l'analyse de plusieurs cas où il y avait conflit entre les objectifs de l'Etat actionnaire et ceux des dirigeants de la corporation, il semble que la capacité qu'a le gouvernement de poursuivre des buts non-commerciaux, à travers les activités d'une CPM, soit très relative. Elle dépendrait de la nature exacte de la relation qui existe entre l'Etat et la CPM, et du degré de réaction d'intérêts non directement associés à la corporation aux tentatives d'influence du gouvernement.

Trois CPM sont examinées dans cette étude: la Corporation de développement du Canada (CDC), Télésat Canada et les détenteurs de titres de la Caisse de dépôt et placement du Québec. Une grande partie des renseignements servant de base à l'analyse des conflits d'objectifs et de leur résolution provient d'interviews personnelles, conduites auprès d'agents officiels des corporations et de l'Etat.

Après avoir établi les limites générales de la CPM, envisagée dans sa capacité d'instument politique, l'étude entreprend d'examiner les particularités de chaque CPM par rapport au rendement social des capitaux publics investis. Celles-ci sont variées et vont du succès relatif de Télésat à promouvoir une capacité domestique accrue dans la fabrication de satellites, à l'assistance concertée que certains détenteurs de titres de la Caisse ont apportée au développement économique du Québec, en passant par les vagues rendements sociaux dont a bénéficié le public canadien, à la suite de ses investissements dans la CDC.

Introduction

Events of the last several years have focused attention on what previously was a little-known aspect of Canada's political economy, the mixed ownership corporation (MOC). After almost a decade of quiescence in the relationship between the federal government and the Canada Development Corporation (CDC), in which Ottawa was the principal shareholder, a major confrontation over control of the CDC developed in 1981. The aftermath was the federal government's decision to sell its shareholding in the corporation. At about the same time the investment activities of the Caisse de dépôt et placement du Québec became a subject of increasing controversy. Indications that the Caisse was pursuing a more active role in relation to some of its private sector shareholdings led to charges that it had become "politicized" under the Parti Québécois government, and even to an abortive attempt by the federal government to impose statutory limits on the investment capacity of provincial governments and their agents. A third development that has contributed to recent academic and governmental interest in the MOC is the "privatization" phenomenon, involving the partial or complete sale of the state's ownership share in a corporation to private investors. Where the divestiture is incomplete or deliberately phased in over time this may be due simply to financial calculations regarding the capacity of the stock market to absorb the share offer (this has been the case in Britain). In some cases, however, divestiture has been incomplete for political reasons, namely, government's desire to maintain an internal channel for influencing corporate behaviour.

The MOC inhabits the murky area between the public and private sectors. Formally defined, an MOC is a commercial operation, generally taking the form of a joint stock company, in which equity and/or representation on the board of directors is shared, in varying ratios, between one or more private investors and the national and/or regional governments, or their agents. The possibility of state representation or other lever of direct influence in the absence of equity is included in this definition because of recent proposals that would see the state retain a "golden share" in certain Crown corporations sold to the private sector. This has been done in the case of some recent privatizations in Britain, and is favoured by some supporters of privatization in France. The state retains a nominal share in the corporation, but that share carries a right of veto regarding specified categories of decisions (for example, foreign takeovers).

Measurement of the extent of mixed enterprise in the Canadian economy presents some problems. The foremost difficulty involves identification of the universe of firms with share capital divided in some ratio between the state and private sector investors. Two recent attempts to catalogue this population of jointly owned corporations offer hugely different estimates of the number of firms falling within this category. Anthony Boardman and his colleagues place the number of mixed enterprises in Canada at over 1,000, a figure that conveys a grossly inflated impression of the size of the mixed capital sector of the economy.[1] This formidable sum is arrived at by including not only corporations in which governments in Canada, directly or through their agents, hold some ownership share, but also the equity investments of these corporations. When one considers that corporations like Canadian Pacific, Macmillan Bloedel and Dominion Textile, each of which accounts for a vast network of subsidiaries, are designated mixed enterprises by the Boardman group, it becomes evident that their operationalization is too inclusive to carry political significance.

Using a more restrictive definition of mixed enterprise, one that does not include corporations that are several stages removed from equity ownership by the state, William Stanbury and Craig Elford place the number of mixed enterprise firms at 292 (1981).[2] Of this number almost a third are accounted for by investments of the Caisse de dépôt et placement du Québec, and another 48 are subsidiary corporations within the Canada Development Corporation's network of holdings.[3] Recognizing that identification is only the starting point for an assessment of the significance of mixed enterprise in the Canadian economy, Stanbury and Elford break down this population by (1) corporation size, and (2) the nature of the state's investment. Correlating these two factors, they find that the vast majority of state investments is accounted for by portfolio investments (i.e., the state's ownership share is too small to carry control) in small and medium-sized corporations. The large number of portfolio investments in large and medium-sized firms, held by provincial governments or their agents, is overwhelmingly due to the investments of a single state agency, Québec's Caisse de dépôt et placement. Caisse investments comprise 68 of the 97 MOCs in the portfolio category. If the equity investments of the Caisse are excluded from this analysis the concentration of mixed enterprises toward the lower end of Canada's corporate hierarchy is even more marked. The results of Stanbury and Elford's analysis are presented in Table I.1.

Stanbury and Elford identify only four cases in which the state shareholder has effective control over a corporation with assets in excess of $500 million. However, with the population of firms defined as the *Financial Post 500* for 1982 (the 500th firm having sales of $46.9 million) they find that 14 of the corporations in this group were mixed enterprises under the legal or effective control of either the federal or a provincial government, or a Crown agent. This compares with 28 federal and provincial Crown corporations in the *Financial Post 500* for that year. Clearly then, mixed ownership firms under state control account for a not insignificant share of corporate activity in Canada. Indeed, Stanbury and Elford estimate that in 1981 state equity in MOCs amounted to 7.5 per cent of total equity capital in Canada, and the assets of those MOCs under the legal or effective control of governments in Canada comprised approximately 5 per cent of all assets of non-financial corporations in Canada for that year.[4]

The central argument of this study is that the MOC involves an ambiguous form of organization that limits the ability of the government shareholder to impose its policy goals on that organization when these seriously conflict with those of management and/or private sector shareholders. This does not mean that the MOC is inherently unworkable, but simply that the fact of private investors to whom management can claim a fiduciary responsibility is a condition that both complicates the accountability relationship between the state and its investments, and which may operate as a defence against the imposition of goals determined by the government. In other words, ownership *does* make a difference by influencing the contingent relationships between various actors, as well as the

Table I.1
Mixed Enterprises[a] – Corporate Size (Revenue) by the Nature of the State's Investment

Size of Firm[b] 1981	Nature of the Investment: Portfolio	Effective Control	50:50 Partnership	Legal Control	Total	
A. Federal government investments						
Large ($500m+)	1	2	0	0	3	
Medium ($50-500m)	5	0	2	2	9	73 (96%)
Small (under $50m)	36	2	17	9	64	
Total	42	4	19	11	76	
B. Provincial government						
Large ($500m+)	47	2	0	0	49	
Medium ($50-500m)	24	2	0	4	30	93 (66%)
Small (under $50m)	26	6	14	17	63	
Total	97	10	14	21	142	

Table I.1 (continued)

a. The discrepancy between the total of 292 firms which Stanbury and Elford place in the mixed enterprise category, and the 218 firms included in this table, is explained by the fact that what they call "second order mixed enterprises" (i.e., the subsidiaries of corporations in which the state holds shares directly, or indirectly through a Crown agent) are excluded.

b. With assets substituted for revenue as a measure of corporate size, the distribution is basically the same. See Table 4 at page 28 in the Stanbury and Elford paper.

c. Stanbury and Elford recognize that the characterization of the state's investments is often a matter of judgement. The 50:50 partnership and legal control (i.e., 51 per cent of voting shares) situations pose no problem, but the difference btween a portfolio investment and effective control is not always clear. Cases where the state investor is the largest minority shareholder, and where the state's ownership share is large enough that effective control is at least conceivable (e.g. the Caisse's 16 per cent share of Dominion Textile, and, at the time of their study, the CDIC's 48 per cent stake in the CDC) have been judged on the basis of their particular circumstances.

Source: Adapted from Tables 3 and 4, pp. 27-28, in C. Elford and W. Stanbury, "Mixed Enterprises in Canada", paper presented to the Seminar on Crown Corporations, Royal Commission on the Economic Union and Development Prospect for Canada, Ottawa, June 1, 1984. With permission of the authors.

opportunities for conflicts to arise and the channels for their resolution.

In this study the partnership of public and private capital in the mixed ownership corporation is examined in order to better understand the possibilities and limitations of the mixed ownership corporation as an instrument of public policy. In describing the factors that have determined government's ability to impose its policy preferences on the MOC, when these preferences conflict with those of managers and/or private shareholders, there is no intention to pass personal judgment on how sensitive or insensitive the MOC *should* be to the government's expectations for corporate behaviour. Rather, the issue being addressed is simply this: Assuming that a government has non-commercial policy goals, how amenable is the MOC as an instrument for the pursuit of these goals?

Of course the same question can be, and has been, asked about wholly state-owned companies and about private businesses that operate as the "chosen instrument" of government. And indeed some of the conclusions arrived at regarding the factors that influence a government's ability to impose its policy preferences on the MOC also apply in some degree to self-financing Crown corporations. A systematic comparison of the MOC, a Crown corporation and a chosen instrument like SPAR would be a necessary prelude to conclusions regarding the relative advantages and disadvantages of these different organizational structures as policy instruments. Such ambitious comparisons are beyond the scope of the present study. This, however, does not preclude general speculation in the concluding chapter about such questions as whether the MOC presents either problems or opportunities for government influence that are different in kind from or simply in degree from those encountered in the case of Crown corporations.

During debate on the legislation establishing PetroCanada, a government spokesman observed that one of the reasons for rejecting the mixed ownership model in favour of a wholly state-owned petroleum company was the desire to avoid creating a Canadian version of British Petroleum, an MOC which has been remarkably indifferent to government preferences at several points in its corporate history. The current popularity of the privatization concept, and the allure of equity sales as a means of raising revenue, may obscure consideration of the less immediate issue of what happens when the preferences of management and the state shareholder come into conflict. If partial privatization of PetroCanada is likely to lead to the sort of relationship between that corporation and public policy experienced in the case of BP or, to invoke Canadian history, if the sale of equity in state enterprises to private investors involves re-creating the Canada Development Corporation model, these decisions should be taken in light of what is known about the MOC. Based on the cases reviewed in the subsequent chapters, there is no reason to assume that all future governments will be content with a passive relationship to its shareholding, nor does the concept of the "golden share," whereby the state shareholder retains a veto over certain decisions (e.g., corporate takeovers or plant closures), represent a sure means of ensuring that the MOC is responsive to government's policy preferences.

The three case studies selected for intensive analysis are the Canada Development Corporation, Telesat Canada, and the private sector investments of the Caisse de dépôt et placement du Québec. The choice of the CDC, Telesat and the Caisse portfolio of companies is deliberate. They represent three organizationally different ways by which the state has entered into partnership with private investors in a single business firm. The organizational differences between these cases, a structural variable, are crucial in a study that sets out to determine the possibilities for, and problems with, the mixed ownership corporation as a policy instrument. Thus, this study examines a case where the state is a shareholder along with a small number of private shareholders in a corporation that operates under special legislation that assigns the state certain privileges in corporate decision-making (Telesat); a case where the state is a shareholder along with thousands of private investors in a corporation that operates under special legislation that assigns the state only limited special rights in corporate decision-making (CDC); and finally a case where the state operates through an investment agency to acquire and hold equity in corporations that operate under general business law (the Caisse's equity portfolio). The structural variable is argued to be one of the significant determinants of the state's ability to act through the MOC in pursuing policy goals that conflict with the preferences of management and private shareholders.

In Chapter 1 the circumstances attending the creation of Telesat and the CDC, and the decision to assign the Caisse an equity investment role, are reviewed. Chapter 2 examines the organizational features of each case, in order to determine how the legal/institutional characteristics of an MOC influence the corporate decision-making process and the state shareholder's relationship to that process. This is followed in Chapter 3 by analysis of several cases of conflict between corporate management and the state shareholder. The focus upon the resolution of conflict should not obscure the fact that the interests of the state and those of private sector actors (shareholders, management, financiers) with which it is associated through the MOC frequently are convergent. This is evident from the analysis in Chapter 4 of the performance of each case as an instrument of public policy. Chapter 5 draws together the lessons that emerge from the Canadian cases reviewed, and speculates on the possibilities for, and limitations of, the MOC as a policy instrument.

The overall conclusion of this study is that government's original expectations of influence on corporate behaviour have been blocked by organizational features of the MOC which involve a mobilization of bias in favour of business values. Managers appear to treat the public policy expectations of the state, where these are not consistent with management's preferences, as unwarranted intrusions upon corporate autonomy, to be resisted as far as possible. Analysis of situations in which conflict surrounded the decisions demonstrates that the price of forced compliance with the state's preferences is crisis in the relationship between the state and private capital in the MOC, while the price of induced compliance is compensation. The state's ability to influence corporate decisions is further complicated by an observed tendency for conflict to spread beyond the bounds of the firm, so that state intervention is perceived to challenge a broader set of business interests than the corporate autonomy and profitability of the MOC. Based on a review of the performance of each case, this study concludes that the social return on the public's invested capital has varied from the relative success of Telesat in promoting the growth of a domestic manufacturing capacity in satellites, through the supportive relationship of the Caisse's equity investments to Quebec's francophone bourgeoisie, to the nebulous social returns on the Canadian public's investment in the CDC.

Moreover, there is evidence that government's expectations for the MOC have been at times naive. This naivety has two dimensions. First is the significance of *private* shareholders, whose rights can be invoked as a protective shield by MOC managers in rejecting the expressed preferences of the government shareholder. Related to that is the observed tendency for managers to value their independence from the influence of the government shareholder. This cannot be explained simply by the background and personal characteristics of MOC managers, although these have reinforced management's resistance to government influence in the particular cases examined in this study. It is in the self-interest of the managers to assert maximum autonomy and minimal responsibility for whatever non-commercial preferences for corporate behaviour that the government shareholder might have. This may be understood more concretely from an example. A government might wish to see an MOC invest in a region characterized by high unemployment. The political benefits, including future voter support, that the government may expect to follow from such behaviour are not benefits that MOC managers share in. An investment in regional development policy that undermines the commercial performance of the MOC could carry adverse consequences for its ability to finance itself from earnings and private sector financial markets. Assuming that the MOC is open to the private sector in two ways, namely, that it is in competition with other firms and that it relies on private investors for part of its capital (which is by definition true of the MOC), it will be in the interest of management to resist (perhaps demanding to be compensated for) government preferences that in management's estimation threaten either the corporation's ability to compete or its independence from the state treasury. Dependence on the state treasury carries greater public accountability for the MOC's actions and thus may transform corporate decision-making from a relatively private matter involving principally management and the board of directors into a matter of public debate in the legislature and perhaps in the media.

Open-ended personal interviews with public servants and MOC managers provide much of the information on which Chapters 2 and 3 are based. In focusing on the significance of the state's ownership participation for corporate decision-making, it was found useful to concentrate on particular instances of reported conflict between the state investor and management of the mixed ownership corporation. This strategy reflects the study's central preoccupation with the possibilities for, and limits on, state capital in the produce-for-profit economy. As an object of analysis the decision-making process is therefore significant to the extent that it affords insight into the effectiveness of the MOC as an instrument of public policy.

Chapter 1

The Ambiguous Organization: Three Forms of the Mixed Ownership Corporation

Proposals for partial, as opposed to complete, privatization of state assets assume that the retention of an ownership share by the state provides a latent lever for *direct* influence on corporate behaviour that may be used in appropriate circumstances. But this assumption that the mixed ownership corporation (MOC) represents a compromise between state ownership and regulation through some less direct form of state intervention is not a product of the privatization debate. It was expressed over 50 years ago by Marshall Dimock, in his suggestion that the MOC represented a possible alternative to administratively cumbersome regulation of utilities. Dimock identified three advantages to the former in comparison to regulation: (1) it allows a direct means for the capture of economic rent (i.e., monopoly profits); (2) the joint stock company organizational form, with the participation of private sector investment, ensures that the corporation will be run as a market-responsive commercial operation; and (3) regulation, with its attendant administrative and arbitrational difficulties, is obviated by the state's day-to-day participation in the management of the enterprise.[1] On the level of ideology, Dimock considered mixed enterprise an effective compromise between laissez-faire economics and socialism.

Dimock's assumption can be stated as a simple proposition:

> The mixed ownership corporation allows for the possibility of direct influence by the state shareholder

> on corporate behavior, while not challenging the general business orientation of the organization.

In other words, the very ambiguity of the MOC, its unconventional character as neither strictly state enterprise nor purely private enterprise, is argued to be its virtue as a policy instrument. Examination of the origins of Telesat, the CDC and the Caisse's equity dimension demonstrates that, to varying degrees, the governments concerned shared this expectation of latent influence.[2]

This is demonstrated most clearly in the case of Telesat. Direct equity participation in the new domestic satellite communications corporation, accompanied by state membership on the board of directors and various approval requirements which, by the terms of the *Telesat Act*, assigned the federal government a pre-eminent role in the board's decision-making, was to provide the state with both a window on developments and levers of control in a sector characterized by unpredictable technological change.

These control provisions included:

1. Section 8, whereby all procurement and construction proposals are subject to review by the minister of communications (though the *Act* is silent about what happens in the event that the Minister does not issue written approval within the specified period)

2. Section 9, whereby all negotiations with foreign states or their agents, and participation within trans-national organizations, must be carried out under the authority of the minister of communications

3. Section 14 (1), whereby the federal government is assigned a veto power in the annual election of Telesat's president

4. Section 20 (2) (3), whereby the transfer of common shares (and therefore any change in Telesat's ownership structure) requires cabinet approval

5. Section 33, whereby a change in the objects of the corporation requires government approval through letters patent.

At the same time the ownership stake of the common carriers provided the industry with a direct channel of participation in the development of the satellite system, and thus satisfied the carriers' interest in protecting their market positions against the inroads of a new technology. In short, the mixed enterprise organizational structure met the demands of both the federal government and the common carriers over the domestic application of this new telecommunications technology.

Even though there were advocates of the Crown corporation option for the satellite company, including the Science Council of Canada, the New Democratic Party and, at one point, the Canadian Broadcasting Corporation, while the common carriers initially took the position that they ought to be assigned exclusive ownership of the new satellite corporation, it would be a distortion to conceive of the mixed ownership choice as a political compromise between these positions. Unlike the earlier case of COMSAT in the United States, the Canadian telecommunications carriers did not possess the political leverage to dictate terms effectively to the government. While the Bell Canada-dominated TransCanada Telephone System (TCTS; now Telecom Canada) paralleled the telecommunications dominance of AT&T in the United States, the structure of political decision-making in Canada (characterized by a dominant executive and a compliant legislature) did not enable the Canadian carriers to control a necessary stage in the policy-making process, in the way that the interests of the AT&T-led telecommunications oligopoly were represented by the United States Senate Aeronautical and Space Sciences Committee.[3] The Canadian carriers were compelled to seek access to the policy-making system at the cabinet level, and their success in acquiring a share of control over the new corporation and the application of satellite technology to domestic telecommunications must be ascribed to three factors.

The first was that the only organizational precedent, namely, that of COMSAT, combined private ownership with state representation on the board of directors. The American government's participation was limited to three presidentially-appointed directors without any ownership share. The report to the Canadian cabinet which made recommendations regarding the organization of the new corporation (*MacIntosh Report*), relied heavily on the American precedent as a model to be followed with some significant adaptations. The second and third factors are less amenable to documentation, but are deductively convincing. The terrestrial telecommunications companies, represented by the TCTS, argued that their massive capital investment, together with the fact that a satellite system would require interconnection with this ground-based infrastructure, argued for direct industry participation in any new domestic satellite corporation. When it became clear that the federal government would not be content with regulatory control over the domestic satellite system, the industry embraced the mixed ownership option as a less than optimal response to its demand for control. It should be remembered that the federal government's technical experience and policy-making capability in telecommunications carriage was limited. The Department of Communications had not even been constituted when the idea of a domestic satellite system reached the political agenda (DOC was created in 1969, the same year as the *Telesat Act* was passed). The carriers' arguments that their research and operational expertise would be necessary for the success of the domestic satellite system and, moreover, that a satellite system would have to be integrated into the existing system of terrestrial telecommunications (owned and operated by the common carriers), were doubtless persuasive in convincing the federal cabinet that direct participation by the carriers was necessary. Finally, in a cabinet that included such supporters of the business community as Mitchell Sharp, C.M. Drury, Alistair Gillespie, John Turner, Edgar Benson and Paul Hellyer, it can be safely assumed that the industry's demands for control received a sympathetic hearing. The government's reluctance to countenance complete ownership of the satellite system by the existing carriers must be attributed to the lessons learned from the COMSAT experience in the United States, namely, that the development of satellite communications would not proceed with dispatch if placed under the control of the carriers and that the right to nominate a minority of the corporation's directors was not an effective lever for government influence.

In adopting a mixed ownership structure for the Canada Development Corporation, the federal government was responding to a very different configuration of actors and demands than that which brought forth Telesat. As a holding company intended to increase Canadian ownership in industrial sectors of the economy, the CDC galvanized more broadly-based opposition. Indeed, uncertainty about what purpose(s) the CDC was to pursue led to general suspicion and trepidation in the business community. Moreover, the CDC involved direct state participation in a part of the economy which, except under unusual circumstances such as the exigencies of wartime, was considered the exclusive preserve of private sector decision-makers. The legitimate bounds of the state's role extended to defining the ground rules regulating activity in the industrial economy (i.e., combines legislation, business law, product standards), and measures in support of private capital accumulation (tariff and non-tariff barriers to foreign competition, industrial assistance through the subsidization of infrastructural requirements). But as demonstrated by perennial demands from the business community for the privatization of Polymer, direct state ownership of commercially viable corporations was considered an illegitimate intrusion upon private sector hegemony in the produce-for-profit sector of the Canadian economy.

The mixed ownership structure of the CDC represented an unequal compromise between two conceptions of the problem of high levels of direct foreign investment in Canada's industrial economy. At the centre of the industrial policy view was the argument that foreign ownership contributed to the underdevelopment of Canada's economy. This was attributed to the production, financing and investment policies of foreign-owned subsidiaries, policies that were shaped to serve the interests of the foreign parent corporation and its shareholders. According to this analysis, a CDC was a necessary part of an industrial policy to repatriate economic decision-making. The advocates of the industrial policy version of the CDC argued for a wholly state-owned investment corporation with a mandate linked to a government policy restricting foreign takeovers of Canadian corporations.

In opposition to this approach was the capital markets version of the CDC proposal, which considered high levels of foreign ownership of Canadian industry to be a problem only to the extent that a disproportionate share of the benefits from economic activity in Canada accrued to non-nationals. According to this view, a CDC would contribute to an expansion in domestic ownership of the Canadian economy by serving as a large pool of equity capital for investment in Canadian industry.

While the capital markets analysis ultimately influenced the CDC legislation, this diagnosis of the problem did not necessarily call for state investment as a policy response. Taxation instruments probably would have been preferred by the Department of Finance, in which the tools of fiscal policy comprised the conventional wisdom on state intervention in the economy. Furthermore, there was general opposition to the CDC concept in the business community, and strong reservations within parts of the governing Liberal Party.[4]

In view of this combination of bureaucratic disinclination and private sector opposition, the government's decision to establish a mixed enterprise investment corporation must be attributed to the political commitment that had developed under successive Liberal governments. The *idea* of the CDC had been a prominent issue on the public agenda from the time of Walter Gordon's nationalistic budget in 1963. While the CDC was never considered a panacea, economic nationalists viewed it as a necessary part of a broader policy of repatriating economic decision-making. The CDC created under Edgar Benson in 1971, although not connected to the government's policy on the foreign takeover of Canadian corporations and lacking an unequivocal industrial development mandate, nonetheless would be a wholly Canadian-owned holding company with a mandate to "help develop and maintain strong Canadian-controlled and managed corporations in the private sector of the economy and (to) give Canadians greater opportunities to invest and participate in the economic development of Canada".[5] Thus, symbolic expression was given to nationalist demands, while at the same time the anticipated participation of private investors appeared to confirm that the CDC would not be a government-controlled instrument of industrial policy.

Several features of the CDC Act made it clear that the proposed corporation was to operate unfettered by formal lines of control by, and accountability to, the federal government. These included:

1. Section 6, which states that the objects of the corporation "shall be carried out in anticipation of profit and in the best interests of the shareholders as a whole," thereby establishing an agent/principal relationship virtually identical to that of a private sector corporation

2. Section 7(e), whereby the corporation is empowered to invest outside of Canada when, *in management's judgment*, such investment is expected to promote the objects of the company

3. Section 13(1), whereby the selection of the corporation's president is the prerogative of the board of directors

4. Section 30(1), especially clauses (a) and (b), whereby the corporation is effectively exempted from the requirement of parliamentary approval for changes in the objects and powers of the company

5. Section 31, stating that the CDC is not an agent of the Crown, and does not fall within the classes of organizations covered by the *Financial Administration Act*

6. Section 40(1), whereby the federal government is given the option of annually appointing up to four of the members of the board of directors, in lieu of voting its shares on resolutions electing members to the board (thereby accepting a lower level of board representation than the government's ownership share would entitle it).

It is probably fair to say that the federal government did not have a clear idea of what its own relationship to CDC decision-making would be. In attempting to satisfy the economic nationalists while not alienating the business community, which was suspicious of the CDC idea, the government laid the basis for misunderstandings that would surface at the end of the 1970s.

The Caisse de dépôt et placement bears a surface similarity to the CDC to the extent that an important expressed rationale for each was to increase "indigenous" ownership of industry in Quebec and Canada respectively. Of course the Caisse was not organized as a mixed enterprise, but as an administratively independent investment agency of the Quebec state. It was, however, assigned a direct investment capacity which, whether measured as a proportion of the Caisse's total assets or in absolute dollar terms, was expected to make the Caisse the largest equity investor in the province, and one of the largest in the country (with growth of the Caisse's assets far in excess of original projections, the Caisse is today *the* single largest equity investor in Canada). With representatives on the board of directors of some of Canada's largest private sector corporations, including Domtar, Noranda and Provigo, the Caisse has become a vehicle for state participation in both the provincial and national economy.

But as the Chapter 3 analysis of the CDC will demonstrate, the accoutrements of control, i.e., a large ownership share and representation on the board of directors, should not be confused with its effective exercise. The legislation establishing the Caisse is silent in regard to what constitutes appropriate participation in the affairs of corporations in which the Caisse is a major shareholder. Unlike either Telesat or the CDC, the Caisse has no "special," i.e., statutorily defined, relationship to its shareholdings. There are no express prohibitions against officers of the Caisse sitting on the board of directors of public companies, and the ceiling on the ownership share which may be held in any single corporation (30 per cent) is, arguably, higher than would have been set if the Caisse was expected to be a passive investor in all circumstances.

As the investor of savings under the Quebec Pension Plan, and other deposits assigned to it by its charter and the provincial government, the Caisse has a clear fiduciary responsibility. But evidence of the Caisse's relationship to provincial economic development is no less certain. Statements of the Lesage government show plainly that the Caisse was expected to be the pivotal institution in the province's economic development. That the Caisse was the trustee of the state-mandated savings of millions of Quebec citizens was not understood to preclude an active investor role for the agency. Within the conditions set down by its charter, the Caisse's management was given wide latitude in determining such matters as the sectoral and regional distribution of equity investments, and participation (through board representation) in corporate decision-making. Under these circumstances the orientation of the Caisse's board of directors and, notwithstanding statutory guarantees of the chairman's independence, the expectations of the government would be key determinants of the agency's equity investment policy.

Direct participation by the Caisse in corporate decision-making is not, therefore, proscribed by the agency's charter nor outside (though admittedly not central to) the expectations held for the Caisse by its founders. *Prima facie*, this participation would appear to compromise private sector decision-making prerogatives in an affected corporation. The challenge which the Caisse poses to corporate autonomy is, however, qualified by the nationalist purposes that the agency represents. This may be expressed as a proposition:

> Direct participation by the Caisse in corporate decision-making (through representation on the board of directors of a publicly-traded company) involves, at minimum, an implicit challenge to private capital accumulation and private sector decision-making hegemony. However, this challenge is directed at non-francophone capital rather than at private capital accumulation and decision-making *per se*.

In other words, certain of the mixed ownership investments of the Caisse may represent an intrusion upon the decision-making prerogatives of the non-francophone private sector, while at the same time contributing to the strength of the francophone business class. This proposition will be examined more closely in subsequent chapters. While generally valid, one must explain the fact that not all segments of Quebec's francophone business community support the Caisse's direct investment activities.

The equity investments of the Caisse represent a much more common form of mixed ownership than the deliberately created MOC that operates under special legislation. Internationally, extensive state shareholdings in publicly-traded corporations are controlled by such investment agencies as France's Caisse des dépôts et consignations, Sweden's state holding company, Statsforetag, and Italy's huge state holding companies, the largest of which are the Istituto per la Recostruzione Industriale (IRI) and Ente Nazionale Idrocarburi (ENI). Both IRI and ENI have been active recently in reducing the state's ownership share in many of their holdings. None of these agencies, however, has privatization as a main function, in the way that the Canada Development Investment Corporation was proclaimed a vehicle for the privatization of state assets when Paul Marshall was appointed its chairman in 1984.

Proposals for the partial privatization of state assets should not approach the MOC as though it were a *tabula rasa* about which little is known. Alternative structures were proposed for CDC and Telesat and the final choice of a mixed ownership structure did not follow inescapably from either their functions or the Canadian tradition of state enterprise. The provincial commission which recommended that the Caisse be created to invest the funds that would be collected under a Quebec Pension Plan drew on the experience of some Western European nations, including France, Belgium and Sweden. Out of the different circumstances surrounding the creation of Telesat, the CDC and the Caisse emerged three very different forms of the partnership between private and public capital. These institutional variations have had important consequences for the relationship between the state shareholder and management of the MOC. The channels for state shareholder influence and the defences available to MOC management are conditioned by institutional features of the corporation. The next three chapters consider the experience of Telesat, the CDC and the private sector shareholdings of the Caisse in order to better appreciate the possibilities and problems of the MOC as an instrument of public policy.

Chapter 2

Structures and Actors: The Inner Life of the Mixed Ownership Corporation

The question of whether ownership makes a significant difference in the behaviour of a corporation is very much an open one and, with some simplification, positions on the matter can be divided into two groups. One group is concerned, first, that state ownership will reduce the competitive performance of the corporation because of the possibility of transfers from the state (thus implicitly operating to limit the discipline of economic markets) and, second, that a government is likely to attempt to impose non-commercial goals on the organization. The theoretical justification for the privatization of state assets is based on the premise that ownership does indeed make a difference.[1] The other group considers the market circumstances of the corporation to be the key factor determining its behaviour and, therefore, views the ownership question as immaterial. This understanding of corporate behaviour assumes that managers, whether of a privately or publicly owned organization, seek to maximize their decision-making autonomy, and that in the case of a state enterprise this is done most effectively by minimizing the organization's financial dependence on the state. This requires profitability and therefore responsiveness to the same constraints as those observed by privately owned corporations. The argument that ownership is largely irrelevant as a determinant of the firm's behaviour was captured in the quip of a former socialist prime minister of France, Pierre Mauroy, about that country's state-dominated banking sector: "We have nationalized the banks, but not the bankers."[2] In fact both internal characteristics of the firm, including ownership, and market circumstances appear to be relevant in explaining corporate behaviour.

Empirical evidence can be adduced in support of each of these positions. For example, PetroCanada invested far more heavily in frontier exploration during its first several years of operation than did the privately owned petroleum corporations, a difference that cannot be understood apart from PetroCanada's early dependence on state transfers before the acquisition of Petrofina gave it an independent cash flow. Canadair and de Havilland, nationalized in the mid-1970s, are classic cases of organizations whose ability to continue producing aircraft in the absence of significant sales, and therefore to continue employing thousands of workers in a labour-intensive high technology industry, must be attributed to the fact of public ownership. On the other hand, the litany of cases where a corporation in which the state was the sole or majority shareholder has behaved in ways largely indistinguishable from its privately owned counterparts, and even cases where state enterprise managers have resisted the imposition of public policy goals that were not consistent with their own preferences for the corporation, is a long one. Conflict between the French government and Air France in the late 1970s over the "nationality" of the state-owned airline's next generation of planes, and with the automobile manufacturer, Renault, over the regional location of new capital investment, are the sort of circumstances that may give rise to such conflicts.[3]

That evidence can be offered in support of both positions on the ownership question demonstrates that the status of an organization as either publicly or privately owned, and the institutional particulars of its relationship to the state, are neither immaterial nor wholly deterministic. These factors are relevant in shaping the decision-making milieu, the structure of cues and perceptions of potential rewards and sanctions within which corporate managers operate. By describing the organizational setting of the decision process in the mixed ownership corporation, this chapter will lay the basis for understanding the cases of conflict examined in Chapter 3.

Structures

(1) The Corporate Charter

From the standpoint of decision-making in the mixed ownership corporation, the provisions of the charter under which the firm operates can be significant in defining both the state's prerogatives as shareholder and the corporation's relationship to public policy. To cite an example from abroad, the corporate charter of the Société Nationale Elf-Aquitaine, a petroleum corporation owned jointly by the French government (67 per cent) and private shareholders, assigns to the state shareholder a right of final approval over major capital spending decisions.[4] A Canadian counterpart to this power of veto over particular classes of decisions is found in Section 8 of the *Telesat Act*, which requires that capital expenditure proposals for satellites and earth stations be submitted to the minister of communications for review before contracts are entered into. The main significance of such a provision lies less in its ultimate exercise (coercive significance) than in the policy signals it provides for management (persuasive significance).

To continue with the case of Telesat, that corporation's charter contains a second provision which, *prima facie*, assigns the government a control prerogative not enjoyed by Telesat's other shareholders. This is Section 14(1) of the act, which provides that cabinet must approve annually the board of directors' selection of Telesat's president. In fact, the corporation has had only two presidents during its 15-year history and there is no evidence that this annual ratification requirement has influenced the behaviour of Telesat management. Indeed, the only consequence of this provision seems to have been that certain legal problems have arisen with respect to the signing of contracts during the period between the expiry of the president's term and his confirmation for a subsequent year. One Telesat principal suggests that the ratification provision *could* operate as a lever of government influence if the president had limited career options. This is a dependent position that has characterized neither of Telesat's presidents.[5]

The CDC, although also incorporated under a special act of parliament, contains no provisions discriminating between the control prerogatives assigned the state as compared to private sector shareholders. Section 40(1), however, gives the government the option of appointing up to four members of the CDC's board of directors annually in lieu of voting its equity in the corporation. This option was exercised by the government until the control crisis of 1981, and represents a remarkable case of legislative provision for the government, as shareholder, to assume voluntarily a decision-making influence that is proportionally much less than, until recently, its ownership share warranted.

Although neither the CDC nor Telesat is an agent of the Crown, a status that is explicitly repudiated in their respective charters and a distinction from Crown corporations on which the management of each corporation has always insisted, the corporate objectives of each make reference to public policy goals. In the case of the CDC, the goals are so general as to have imposed no significant limitation on the corporation's investment latitude. Moreover, there is no indication in the act of the relative emphasis that should be placed on different sectors of economic activity, although the government publicly expressed certain expectations in establishing the CDC.[6] From conversations with management actors it is clear that the only part of the section on corporate objectives that has had any relevance in decision-making is the directive that the CDC's operations "shall be carried out in anticipation of profit and in the best interests of the shareholders as a whole."[7] This provision was invoked as a shield in defending the corporation from charges that it has been insensitive to the industrial policy expectations of its principal shareholder.

A rather similar use of the section on objectives is found in the case of Telesat. When asked about the goals of the satellite corporation, a number of Telesat actors referred to Section 5(1) of the corporation's charter, which states that Telesat is to operate a domestic telecommunications system "on a commercial basis" and that the promotion of a domestic manufacturing capacity in satellites (which is also stipulated in Telesat's corporate objectives) shall be "to the extent practicable and consistent with its commercial nature." This is interpreted by management as a mandate for profitable operation and therefore provides it with a lever in negotiations with the government over Canadian content in satellite procurement decisions. One Telesat actor expressed the view that the public policy objectives set forth in the 1968 White Paper on satellite communications were compromised because of the emphasis placed on commercial operation in the act that was eventually passed.[8] This view was echoed by another management actor who said, "The ancillary social goals of Telesat are quite secondary. In fact, the social and nation-building goals are misconstrued".[9] As a *practical* matter it is true that management has had to settle for weak commercial performance, but this has been to some degree because of the Canadian Radio-Television and Telecommunications Commission's perception of Telesat when making rate decisions.

The fact of incorporation under special legislation, with the federal government controlling 50 per cent of the corporation's equity and with the reference (albeit ambiguous) in the charter to public policy goals, may have been a disadvantage in Telesat's relationship to the Canadian Radio-Television and

Telecommunications Commission. Management actors argue that the CRTC has conceived Telesat as a public service corporation, a misconception that has resulted in rate decisions that have compromised the commercial viability of the satellite company. In other words, the special charter and mixed ownership structure of the corporation are cues that have signalled to the CRTC, the body responsible for setting the rates charged to Telesat's clients, that the corporation is not pre-eminently a profit-oriented enterprise in competition with other telecommunications carriers. Management actors suggest that privatization of the government's ownership share should remove the ambiguity in Telesat's status and compel the CRTC to apply the same rate-of-return standards used in the case of Bell Canada, B.C. Telephone, and CN/CP Telecommunications (all of which are regulated by the CRTC). At issue is what constitutes a "fair" or "reasonable" rate of return on shareholder equity, and it is here that Telesat actors suggest that the corporation's anomalous status has contributed to rate board decisions which are based on a misunderstanding of Telesat's relationship to the government. Indeed, cabinet varied CRTC decisions in 1977 and again in 1981, each time demonstrating support for Telesat management's view of the necessary conditions for commercial viability, in opposition to the CRTC's view of the public interest.

While both Telesat and the CDC are incorporated under special legislation, the private sector corporations in which the Caisse holds equity are incorporated under general business law. In this latter case there is certainly no question of the state, as shareholder, possessing special ownership prerogatives. In fact the experience of the Caisse, in seeking representation on the board of directors of such corporations as CP, Dominion Textile and Alcan, has been that the spirit of the *Canada Business Corporations Act* with respect to board representation of major shareholders in a publicly-traded company is contravened when the Caisse is refused representation that generally would be accorded a private sector investor with an equity share of equivalent size. The formal equality of shareholders under the *CBCA* has not prevented what is, *de facto*, discriminatory treatment of the Caisse as shareholder, because of private sector uneasiness over the relationship between that investment agency and the economic policy of the Quebec government.

(2) The Joint-Stock Company

A joint-stock company may take two forms. The first involves relatively few owners, and shares in the business are not traded on the stock exchange. In law this is referred to as a partnership.

The second is the publicly-traded business corporation, arguably the institution most representative of capitalism in the 20th century. The CDC and the private sector equity investments of the Caisse fall into this second category, while Telesat, notwithstanding the original intention to sell shares to the public, remains a partnership between the federal government and 13 telecommunications corporations (with Bell Canada holding a 25 per cent ownership share).

With the two exceptions of silent partner status (under which a party contributes equity to a closely-held company without receiving the right to control prerogatives) and that of non-voting equity issued by a publicly-traded company, equity carries both voting rights and an expectation, enforceable in law, that management will exercise reasonable judgment in protecting the investment of the corporation's shareholders. In general there are no legal limitations on the state's capacity to purchase equity in a private sector corporation, except for the legislative provisions that regulate the investment activities of particular state agencies like the Alberta Heritage Savings Trust Fund and the Caisse. Nonetheless, while the state as investor has in law the same rights as a private sector shareholder, the fiduciary responsibility of management to the firm's *shareholders as a whole* and, in the case of a publicly-traded company, the ready transferability of ownership shares on the stock exchange, are factors that complicate the state's equity involvement in a joint-stock company.

The 1981 confrontation between the federal government and the CDC over control of that corporation, described in the next chapter, provided a dramatic lesson in the limitations of the public company as a policy instrument. In the words of one company official: "After the experience of May 1981, the government learned something about public companies. The government came to realize the problem of fitting into a public company, and this led to the decision to establish the CDIC as a vehicle for managing, and eventually divesting, the government's holding in the CDC."[10] In the view of CDC management, the federal government *could not* have opposed the board of directors and elected Maurice Strong as chairman of the corporation. Politically, the government might have decided to risk whatever fallout would have ensued from such a move. But its demand that Strong be installed as chairman was, according to some CDC actors, untenable from a legal point of view. Not only had the incumbent chairman been duly appointed under a two-year contract, but the assertion of the government's voting power (48 per cent of CDC equity) under these circumstances would have raised the legal question of whether the rights of the shareholders *as a whole*, as described in Section 6 of the act, were compromised by such an action. The period from the CDC's refusal to invest in Massey-Ferguson to the failed effort to instal Maurice Strong as chairman and increase the government's voting representation on the board of directors, represented a steep learning curve whereby the federal government came to realize that a decade of non-interference in CDC affairs had simply reinforced the implicit limits on state control that were inherent in the public company.

Investment in the shares of a publicly-traded corporation is regulated by a complex set of rules, administered by the securities commission of the province in which a transaction occurs. The 1981 takeover of Domtar by the Caisse and another agent of the Quebec state, the Société générale de financement (SGF), raised the question of whether the state is subject to the same rules as a private sector investor. After reviewing the trading activity which culminated in the effective takeover of Domtar, the Ontario Securities Commission (OSC) observed that the Caisse had committed two transgressions. The first involved a violation of the Caisse's own charter, which proscribes it from holding more than 30 per cent of the equity of any single corporation[11] (a violation which, presumably, ought to have been of greatest concern to the Quebec government). More relevant to the question of whether the Crown is bound by the same investment rules as private sector investors was the OSC's judgment that the Caisse had made a takeover bid which, under the terms of the legislation governing share trading in Ontario, required a public offer to all shareholders. These circumstances brought to a head the issue of public disclosure of investment transactions, and led the OSC to suspend the Caisse from trading on the Toronto Stock Exchange. The Caisse's position was that as an agent of the Crown it was not bound by the disclosure requirements attendant upon share trading. Until all Crown corporations were required by law to observe these regulations, the Caisse was not prepared to be more forthcoming in filing trading reports.[12]

At issue is whether the investment activity of the state, through public sector agencies like the Caisse, should be subject to the same controls that regulate private sector investors. The purpose of these controls is to protect the rights of shareholders in publicly-traded corporations, rights that could be prejudicially affected in the absence of full disclosure. In failing to comply with the rules governing investors generally, a state agency may indeed be acting in the interests of its principal. This was the case in the Domtar takeover, where a public offer to all shareholders (which the OSC maintains was required under the *Ontario Securities Commission Act*) would have increased the cost of acquiring control. While circumvention of trading regulations behind the shield of Crown status may be understandable for either financial or political reasons, or both, failure to abide by the ground rules that regulate private sector investors points up the anomalous status of the state as an investor in private sector corporations.

As demonstrated by the sharp decline in the value of CDC shares during the control confrontation of May 1981 and by a similar fall in the value of Domtar shares after the announcement of the joint Caisse/SGF takeover of Domtar, state investment in a publicly-traded company is complicated by the perceptions of other shareholders as reflected in the market value of the corporation's shares. Thus, CDC decision-making in regard to equity financing has been influenced significantly by the fact that the government has been the corporation's principal shareholder. Management's recognition of the relationship between the marketability of CDC shares and investment community perceptions about the likelihood of government intervention in the affairs of the corporation resulted in regular avowals of corporate autonomy, and periodic assurances from the government (usually timed to coincide with a public share offering) that it would refrain from exercising its legitimate rights as the corporation's largest shareholder.

CDC actors suggest that ambivalence in the investment community's reaction to CDC equity issues was dispelled by the time of the corporation's second public share issue in 1980. In the words of one actor: "The irony is that it was just after the successful marketing of the second share issue that the government made its abortive attempt to pitchfork in Maurice Strong (as chairman), without really thinking of the rights of the thousands of private sector shareholders who had purchased shares partly on the strength of a share prospectus which assured non-intervention by the government."[13] Consequently, when the corporation drew up a preliminary share prospectus in March 1983, the issue of the CDC's relationship to the government had to be addressed once again. The prospectus included the complete exchange of letters between Senator Jack Austin, who at the time was the minister responsible for the government's interest in the CDC, and Anthony Hampson, president of the corporation. At the centre of this correspondence was the decision to create the Canada Development Investment Corporation as an instrument for the divestiture of the government's interest, "as soon as the markets are favourable and a reasonable investment return is available,"[14] intended to provide an unequivocal signal confirming the CDC's corporate autonomy.

The equity market does not represent a decision-making constraint in the case of closely-held joint-stock companies, except when there is an intention to issue shares at some point in the foreseeable future, in which case the anticipated reactions of investors must be taken into account in decision-making. In the case of Telesat, the fact that the corporation's shares are not traded publicly has meant that one pressure for competitive performance has been lacking. With the federal government's expectations for Telesat apparently limited to the backward linkages to the satellite manufacturing industry which flow from capital expenditures, and the common carriers satisfied to keep Telesat as it is, namely, neither a competitive threat nor a source of benefits, Telesat management has not been subject to profitability pressures from the corporation's shareholders. One actor said: "With no growth and profitability pressures from either the government or the carriers, this puts a huge onus on management for corporate development.... Management is on its own in determining the long term role and future of Telesat."[15]

Actors

(1) The Board of Directors

While in law a corporate director's sole responsibility is to take reasonable care that the interests of the shareholders as a whole are protected by the decisions of the board, "directors can protect whomever they choose – organizations or external constituency – depending on their own needs and the pressures to which they are subject."[16] As demonstrated in the 1981 confrontation between the CDC and the federal government over the government's representation on the board of that corporation, and in the reluctance of CP, Alcan, and Dominion Textile to concede Caisse demands for representation, the board of directors of a mixed ownership corporation occasionally can become both a forum for the resolution of divergent public sector/private sector preferences and itself a stake in such conflicts. In the case of Telesat, the latent tension between competing shareholder interests is worked out in a less confrontational manner, although the peculiar membership of the corporation's board sensitizes management to considerations that would divide directors.

Telesat's board of directors brings together government appointees, including representatives of the Department of Communication (DOC) and the CBC, and various interests in the telecommunications industry, some of which are in competition for the same markets. Having directors from competing organizations (e.g., Telecom Canada and CN/CP in their conflict over the issue of interconnection[17]) means that management cannot bring certain questions before the board. One management actor mentioned the case of a contract under Telesat's membership in Telecom Canada. It involved competition with CN/CP, which has a representative on Telesat's board of directors.[18] Perhaps more important as a source of latent conflict is that expansion of Telesat's market share in long distance communication or service diversification could threaten a number of the corporation's shareholders. These two conflicts of interest, between Telesat shareholders on the one hand, and between Telesat and its shareholders on the other, led one management actor to observe: "If the government expects us to compete as a retailer in the telecommunications industry it must change the shareholder composition of our board which, currently, involves obvious conflicts of interest."[19]

A long-time director of Telesat expressed the view, confirmed by all the Telesat actors interviewed, that with the exception of the 1976 decision to enter the TCTS (opposed by the CN/CP official on Telesat's board) there has never been any problem in reconciling apparent conflicts of interest at the level of the board of directors.[20] In a limited sense Telesat does, in fact, appear to operate as a vehicle for organizing consensus in the telecommunications industry, at least with respect to the role of satellite carriage within the Canadian communications network. The composite character of the corporation's board, including customers, shareholders, and potential competitors, enables Telesat to fulfill this role, a role that was anticipated in the initial decision to organize Telesat as a mixed ownership corporation. The successful performance of this function, however, requires that Telesat not pose a competitive threat to any of the common carriers, a condition that was part of Telesat's terms of entry into the TCTS.[21]

As a forum for reconciling the sometimes conflicting preferences of the state as shareholder and those of management and private sector shareholders, Telesat's board of directors is overshadowed by less formalized channels of interaction. One management actor insisted, "We have never negotiated with the government through the medium of government directors: we have always consulted directly with the minister of communications and his deputy."[22] Supporting this view that the board is of minor importance as a forum in which the government's preferences for Telesat are expressed and accommodated, is the assessment of a government appointee to the board. This individual indicated that the government had never expressed its preferences on satellite procurement or other decisions through him, and suggested that the government view must have been channelled through the bureaucratic DOC member of the board ("...although DOC board members have always argued that they were speaking in their personal capacity as a Telesat director, as company law requires, rather than as an agent of the government."[23]). Government representation on Telesat's board of directors, particularly through the DOC member, is simply one window on the corporation's decision-making, and not even the most important one.

In the case of the CDC, the federal government's general lack of concern with the corporation's activities during the first 10 years of its operating history was reflected in the irregular attendance at board meetings of the government's *ex officio* members, the deputy ministers of Finance and Industry, Trade and Commerce (IT&C),[24] and the fact that it was the usual practice for lower-ranking officials to substitute for the deputy ministers.[25] This changed after the Liberal Party returned to power in 1980. The senior assistant deputy minister of finance, A.S. Rubinoff, attended CDC board meetings as the government's representative, and the deputy minister, Dr. Ian Stewart, attended board meetings in 1981, the year of heightened conflict in the government-CDC relationship.

This higher level of government representation at CDC board meetings did not, however, signify greater influence in the corporation's decision-making. In a management-controlled holding company like the CDC, the board operates to approve or censure the pattern of decisions made by management. Particular choices and overall corporate strategy are the preserve of management. During CDC's first few years, meetings with the minister of finance (until the 1975 public share offering, the corporation's sole shareholder) were annual, albeit perfunctory, occurrences, held in order to meet the letter of the CDC's charter.[26] These meetings could hardly be said to have provided the federal government with an effective "window" on CDC decision-making, nor was the irregular attendance of the government's *ex officio* board members a channel whereby the largest shareholder's preferences were expressed.[27] In any case the prevailing government view during these years, centred in the Department of Finance, was that the CDC's corporate autonomy should be maintained, both because the corporation was not understood to be a policy instrument and because a record of non-interference by government was considered necessary if the corporation was eventually to issue shares to the public.

As in the case of Telesat, government preferences were never expressed through the state shareholder's representatives on the board. Generally, requests that the CDC consider investing in a particular corporation were made informally by officials in IT&C. In exceptional instances such as Canadair and de Havilland in the mid-1970s, and then Massey-Ferguson in 1980, an investment proposal emanated from cabinet, communicated through a deputy minister.[28] But it was not until the 1981 issue of the chairmanship of the CDC and increased government representation on the board (an issue that was perceived as an unprecedented challenge to corporate autonomy) that the government communicated its preferences through its *ex officio* board members, specifically the deputy minister of finance. Even then, informal channels of communication (telephone conversations between the minister of finance and various CDC directors, media reports of cabinet dissatisfaction with the corporation's investment policy and of the government's intention to propose Maurice Strong for the chairmanship) were important in expressing the government's preferences before these were formally stated to the board by Ian Stewart.

The crisis that culminated in the confrontation between the federal government and the corporation at a CDC board meeting on May 21, 1981, elevated the significance of the board of directors both as a stake and an actor in the decision-making process. As an actor, the directors were unanimous in opposing the government's demands that Maurice Strong be installed as chairman and that two additional government nominees be appointed to the board. That decision was crucial in protecting corporate autonomy. The confrontation demonstrated that the normally passive board of directors of this management-controlled corporation could, in time of crisis, be mobilized as a decisive force in resisting an increase in the influence of the CDC's principal shareholder. The federal government could have forced the issue by voting its equity, but this would have produced a Pyrrhic victory.

Board representation has also been a matter of contention between the Caisse and management of some of its private sector investments. Indeed, much of the private sector's hostility toward the Caisse is attributable to the agency's policy of placing representatives on the board of directors of the firms in which it holds a large ownership share. Caisse officials maintain that the agency has no threshold level at which board representation is sought, but that their policy is flexible across investments, depending on such factors as the expected duration of the Caisse's investment and the proportion of equity held by the Caisse. The rejection by Dominion Textile, Alcan, and CP in 1981-1982 of Caisse requests to be represented on their boards of directors, led to a reassessment of the Caisse's method of acquiring representation. Instead of the pattern observable in the CP and Domtex cases, where the Caisse made a rapid and significant increase in its share of equity and then approached corporate management with a request that the Caisse be accorded the right to nominate members to the board of directors, one Caisse official observed, "There are other ways to get representation on the board". In explaining the Caisse's approach, this official pointed to the way in which the membership of a corporate board of directors is usually decided upon:

> One can't simply point to a board and say, "Well he is their representative, and he is our representative," and so on. A particular board may be proposed to us as a major shareholder, and we will indicate whether we are satisfied or whether we have reservations. At other times we will directly nominate candidates.[29]

This suggests that methods followed in seeking board representation have become more subtle since 1981. Indeed, it is arguable that the Caisse's record of non-interference in the management of Domtar since the 1981 takeover has contributed to an increased receptivity of the agency's claim to representation.[30]

At the time of the Senate committee hearings on the proposed Shareholding Limitation Act, it was estimated that the Caisse had representation on the boards of approximately 15 public companies.[31] In some instances the Caisse is represented directly. Denis Giroux, the Caisse's manager of equity investments, sits on the boards of Brascade Resources, Vidéotron, Noranda, and Sceptre Resources, all of which are Caisse shareholdings. Former officials of the Caisse continue to hold directorships on the boards of several Caisse investments. For example, Carmand Normand, formerly vice-president, sits on the board of Trust Général. Philippe Girard, until recently a portfolio manager with the Caisse, is a director of Gaz Métropolitain. In other cases representation is achieved through directors who are sympathetic to the Caisse's views as shareholder. For example, Fernand Paré, a director of the Caisse, sits on the board of Noranda Mines, which is controlled by Brascade Resources (a partnership in which Brascan holds 70 per cent ownership, and the Caisse 30 per cent). Roger Charbonneau, president of Laboratoires Anglo-French Ltee., is a director of Rolland Inc., chairman of the board of Gaz Métropolitain, and a director of the Régie des rentes. As a final example, Yves Pratt, a Montreal-based lawyer known to have had close ties with the PQ government, became chairman of the board of Domtar in December 1982 and is a director of Power Financial Corporation, in which the Caisse is a partner.[32]

The extent and nature of Caisse participation in corporate decision-making through representation on boards of directors have varied with the circumstances of the investment. An example of active involvement in the affairs of Caisse holdings was provided in the merger of three small food retailing corporations into Provigo, a reorganization that was spearheaded by the Caisse and congruent with the provincial government's policy of encouraging, through merger, the creation of more scale-efficient corporations in the Quebec economy.[33] While this intervention was unusual in its degree, it demonstrates the sort of circumstances that could compel the Caisse to play an active part in decision-making by its investments. More generally, Caisse officials insist that juggling two fiduciary roles (i.e., the Caisse's responsibility to contributors to the Quebec Pension Plan and other citizens whose contributions are invested through the Caisse, and the responsibility to a corporation's shareholders incumbent on any member of a public company's board of directors) and an acknowledged provincial economic development role may seen problematic in theory, but has posed no problem in practice.[34]

The fact that the Caisse views board membership as a means of expressing and protecting the agency's preferences for its holdings, is confirmed by the statement of a high level Caisse official: "We at the Caisse don't want honorary board members, and we don't support the idea of non-voting participation or companies controlled solely by officers."[35] Representation is not sought as an end in itself but as a means of sensitizing a corporation to the provincial economic development goal that, within the constraint of the Caisse's fiduciary role as the investor of various compulsory contribution programmes, forms an acknowledged part of the agency's mandate. In acquiring board representation the Caisse contributes to the achievement of a goal expressed by former Finance Minister Jacques Parizeau and the PQ government, namely, state representation on the boards of directors of major private sector corporations operating in the Quebec economy. Although Quebec's current Liberal government takes a less interventionist line and has even begun the privatization of some state assets, this representation goal has not been expressly repudiated.

Given that the Caisse's nominees are typically members of Quebec's francophone business class, the process of Caisse influence through the board of directors of a private sector corporation is clearly more complex than participation through a delegate. And aside from the Caisse-inspired reorganization of Quebec's food retailing sector through merger leading to the creation of Provigo, it is difficult to isolate specific cases where Caisse representation on the board of directors of a private sector corporation has been used to influence particular corporate decisions. With representation being "indirect" (through members of the francophone business class who are considered sympathetic to the economic nationalism goals promoted by the Caisse), and Caisse decision preferences being general rather than specific (in other words, that the indicative economic policy signals of the Quebec government figure as a constraint in corporate decision-making, not that *particular* investment or production decisions be taken), the board of directors of a public company is not likely to be transformed into a forum for the reconciliation of sometimes conflicting public and private sector goals simply because of Caisse representation. Caisse influence through representation on a corporation's board of directors is subtle; one senior official of the Caisse observed: "Certainly a corporation like Noranda is made more sensitive to provincial economic interests because of the Caisse's ownership participation."[36]

Confirming the general rule that the board of directors acquires elevated significance during transition periods in a corporation's history, the Caisse/SGF takeover of Domtar precipitated an extended period of conflict on the board of this corporation. In the words of one state official:

> It took a full year to establish an effective and cooperative working relationship at the board level, and two years to get business community acceptance for Domtar under state control.... We required a full year to convince outside members of the Domtar board that the corporation would be run according to private sector business principles, and free from government pressure.[37]

The period of crisis on Domtar's board of directors was marked by the resignation of several members, but no major changes were made in corporate management, and this undoubtedly helped to allay private sector fears that Domtar would become a policy instrument of the Quebec state.

(2) Management

The choice of management personnel has reinforced the development of both the CDC and Telesat along private sector lines and away from a policy instrument orientation. In each case management has been consistently unreceptive to shared control with the government to a degree that is not attributable solely to the limitations imposed by the joint-stock company organizational structure.

The manager in a mixed ownership corporation, like his counterpart in a commercially-oriented Crown corporation, may occupy an ambiguous position. Ambiguity will exist when different principals hold contradictory expectations for the organization, a situation requiring management to select from a number of signals (including their own presumed interest in corporate autonomy) when making decisions. Catherine Eckel and Aidan Vining have suggested that the structurally ambiguous position of managers in government-controlled enterprises that are assigned both profitability and public policy objectives, causes tension in managers. They write:

> There is some evidence that managers in these firms develop a form of "organizational cognitive dissonance".... This appears to be particularly problematic when government "instructions" on social objectives are vague, conflicting (i.e., different "suggestions" from different ministries), changing, or implicit. It appears that many joint enterprises resolve the dissonance by concluding that profitability is not important.[38]

Interviews with several management actors from both Telesat and the CDC provided no support for the suggestion that MOC managers find problematic the sometimes conflicting signals produced by the firm's relationship to both government and private capital. It was found that the existence of ambiguity provides an opportunity for management to affirm the commercial goals of the organization, and that cross-pressures are never experienced as role conflict (i.e., psychological tension). Part of the explanation for managers' selective attention to commercial and organizational objectives, and unreceptiveness to the preferences expressed occasionally by the state shareholder, lies in the private sector cast of thought that characterizes the individuals who have managed the CDC and Telesat.

Managers of both corporations expressed deep scepticism about government as a decision-maker. Capturing a consensus shared by all the managers interviewed, one CDC official observed:

> The policy process in government is too slow, too cumbersome, always catching up with reality, and invariably too late. These are the unavoidable pitfalls of political decision-making; but no commercial enterprise could hope to be viable with decision-making characterized by such conditions.[39]

Similar views, frequently accompanied by disdain for the government's preferences, were expressed by all managers. When asked whether the French experience with joint public/private ownership and decision-making through such corporations as Société Nationale Elf-Aquitaine (a case with which CDC actors were quite familiar) demonstrated that joint control is not, *ipso facto*, impossible, some CDC officials suggested that cross-cultural differences in private sector expectations for the state are such that relationships not uncommon in France and other western European countries are unworkable in Canada.[40]

Even though the CDC and Telesat were established under special legislation, with the federal government as the sole shareholder during the first years of each corporation's operation, the government's choice of managers was in neither case based upon a calculation that the chief executive officer (CEO) selected would be sympathetic to government participation in corporate decision-making. In the case of the CDC, the government initially appointed Anthony Hampson as chairman and Marshall Crowe as president, thereby reflecting its own uncertainty about the future development of the corporation. Hampson and Crowe each had careers that straddled the public and private sectors. Hampson had been with the Department of Finance and worked for the Gordon and Porter royal commissions before re-entering the private sector with Power Corporation. The main part of Crowe's career had been devoted to the public sector, with External Affairs and then the Privy Council Office, although he spent six years as an economic adviser with the Canadian Imperial Bank of Commerce. One senior economic official in the federal government maintains that the early conflict of views within cabinet over the relationship of the CDC to government policy was paralleled in a split between Crowe and Hampson.[41] Whether or not this was the case, Hampson officially assumed the positions of president and CEO by May 1973, and Crowe resigned from the board of the corporation in October of that year.

Hampson's private sector background in finance and in the management of a major Canadian holding company was in accord with the Department of Finance conception of how the CDC ought to be managed, i.e., as a private sector corporation that happened to be started with government seed money. The involvement of individuals drawn from the business community was considered vital to establish the CDC's credibility as a commercially-oriented investor. This was an important consideration in view of the business community's scepticism that the corporation would be able to operate free from government interference. One could speculate that the CDC might have developed differently if Maurice Strong, acknowledged to have been the chief architect of the first draft of the CDC legislation that went before cabinet in 1969, and originally expected to head the corporation before he accepted a position as undersecretary with the United Nations, had been involved in the CDC's early operation. Under Hampson's direction, management has been unequivocal in its commitment to corporate growth and profitability. The legitimate bounds of federal government involvement in the CDC were, in the view of management actors, limited to the original provision of capital and the fact that the corporation was established under special legislation (the most salient provision of which, for CDC officials, always has been the section anticipating a reduction in the government's ownership share to 10 per cent). The experience of joint public/private ownership of the CDC has reinforced management's scepticism about the state as an investor. One management actor said, "Seed money is appropriate, but government is bound to conflict with the private sector in decision-making."[42] As an experiment in developing inter-sectoral understanding and accommodation, the CDC has been unsuccessful.

The marginally greater receptivity of Telesat management to the preferences of the government as shareholder appears to have been due to the backward industrial linkage provisions of the *Telesat Act* (sections 5(2) and 8(1) (2)), a structural factor, and not at all due to greater management sympathy with the policy instrument conception of the satellite corporation. The first president of Telesat, David Golden, had previously been a deputy minister in the Department of Industry. Despite his public service background, Golden's approach to the government's interest in the corporation consistently was that public policy objectives were secondary to the commercial goals of Telesat, and where conceded should be treated as recompensable costs. This attitude had early consequences when Telesat management, supported by the board of directors, resisted the government's preference for Canadian-based RCA in the first satellite acquisition decision.[43]

Golden's successor as president (in April 1980) was Eldon Thompson, formerly president of New Brunswick Telephone, a subsidiary of Bell Canada and a shareholder in Telesat. Thompson's involvement in Canada's domestic satellite system goes back to the late 1960s when he worked on studies attempting to demonstrate the uncompetitiveness of satellite technology for most telecommunication markets. Since becoming Telesat's president in 1980, Thompson has been publicly critical of CRTC rate decisions which, he maintains, have constituted the main obstacle to the corporation's expansion into profitable commercial markets. Like Golden before him, Thompson expresses no ambivalence over whether Telesat is a public service with a mandate to operate "on a commercial basis," or a commercial enterprise for which the state shareholder has limited public policy expectations (relating to capital expenditure, not markets) that can be accommodated in exchange for the payment of Canadian content premiums. The second characterization describes Telesat's relationship to public policy, as policy is defined by the government, although management argues that the CRTC's regulatory treatment of the corporation has been based on the former conception of Telesat.[44]

As in the case of the CDC, public policy expectations, whether expressed by the state as shareholder or regulator, are experienced as pressures from outside the organization. The private sector orientation of management contributes in both cases to a defensive attitude toward the state shareholder. In neither case does management consider joint public/private decision-making workable in practice, and corporate autonomy is for all managers a foremost value. These attitudes *reinforce* the structural limitations which the joint stock company organizational structure places on state participation in corporate decision-making.

Summary: The Organizational Setting for Decision-Making

The decision process in the mixed ownership corporation is mediated by the particular organizational features of the firm. Taken together these features involve a mobilization of bias that puts the state shareholder at a disadvantage vis-à-vis private capital in corporate decision-making. While the state's capacity to influence the outcome of decisions varies between MOCs, being greatest where the corporation operates under legislation which ascribes to the state shareholder special rights in regard to particular classes of decisions (as in the case of Telesat), generalization across the CDC, Telesat, and the major private sector corporations in the Caisse portfolio is possible in two areas.

The first relates to the argument of cognitive dissonance advanced by Eckel and Vining. The present study finds no evidence that managers of the mixed ownership corporation have at any time experienced ambivalence in their role as a result of the sometimes divergent expectations of the state shareholder and private capital. If cognitive dissonance is intended to signify the phenomenon of cross-pressures from the corporation's shareholders, then the term is singularly inappropriate. If, on the other hand, it signifies the identification of management actors with a particular set of values when identification with some other set(s) of values is at least possible, in order to avoid ambiguity and confusion in decision-making, a meaning consistent with the psychological studies on cognitive dissonance, this does appear to happen in the MOC. Cross-pressures that managers occasionally are subject to are dealt with by treating the public policy expectations of the state shareholder (where these do not coincide with management's own preferences for corporate behaviour) as intrusions upon corporate autonomy, to be resisted as far as possible or, if the cost of resistance is perceived as too high, to be accommodated with compensation (i.e., treated as an exceptional concession, rather than a matter of course). None of the managers interviewed gave any indication that he perceived his own role, or the relationship of his corporation to the market, to be affected because the state is a major shareholder. Management actors do not view themselves as representatives of the state and the goals that a government might entertain for the MOC. Their responsiveness to the state's public policy expectations is not produced by the partial assimilation of a state agent role, but by coercion or management's perception that complete resistance could result in greater costs than negotiation and accommodation.

It may be that in some circumstances managers anticipate the reaction of the state shareholder, and thus their decisions are influenced in subtle ways which, for methodological reasons, are difficult to observe. Analysis of this unobtrusive influence is hampered by the practical difficulties in studying non-events. But even where there are grounds for suspecting subtle influence, the public policy preferences of the state are experienced as pressures external to management decision-makers, rather than as a schizophrenic role perception.

The second generalization suggested by this analysis is that the partnership of public and private capital in a single firm is influenced by prevailing norms about the business firm in a capitalist society. Specifically, the corporation is viewed as a market-responsive organization for the pursuit of essentially private ends (i.e., shareholders' dividends, employees' career chances and incomes). The *social* dimension of the firm exists insofar as Adam Smith's metaphor of the "invisible hand" finds its modern restatement in the microeconomic orthodoxy, philosophically utilitarian, that the impersonal working of the market is the best means of maximizing social welfare. According to this view, failures in economic performance, which become manifest in social problems such as unemployment and declining industries, are caused by imperfect competition. The answer to monopolistic tendencies is not necessarily less state intervention, but that the state do nothing to compromise the foundation stone of the capitalist economy, namely, the profit oriented firm.

The values that appertain to the corporation in a liberal capitalist society, particularly profitability and organizational autonomy, represent important limits on the state's ability to act through a mixed ownership firm in pursuit of goals that challenge the principle of private capital accumulation. These values provide support for managers' assertion of autonomy from the state shareholder, autonomy that can be defended with reference to the interests of private shareholders and/or the terms of the corporation's charter. This is demonstrated more concretely from the analysis in Chapter 3 of situations surrounding particular decisions that involve conflict between the preferences of the state and private sector stakeholders in the MOC.

Chapter 3

Conflict and its Resolution: Cases of Divergent Expectations for the Mixed Ownership Corporation

It is not difficult to imagine scenarios in which the behaviour of a corporation like PetroCanada, if partially privatized, could lead to conflict between the state shareholder and private investors. Such conflicts, periodic though they have been, have been documented in the case of Britain's mixed ownership oil company, British Petroleum, and the French state's shareholdings in this sector, la Compagnie Française de Pétroles (CFP) and la Société Nationale Elf-Aquitaine (SNEA).[1] The factors that may contribute to such a divergence in preferences for the MOC are various and, as the subsequent analysis will suggest, unpredictable. For example, a change in government or in the overall circumstances of the economy, or of that sector of the economy in which the MOC operates, may alter the expectations held for the MOC by the state shareholder.

The decision to transform a state-owned asset into a MOC when full privatization is financially possible (i.e., there are buyers at an acceptable price for all of the corporation's equity) implies, at a minimum, reluctance to foreclose the possibility of direct influence on the corporation. An alternative to retaining an ownership share might involve eliciting from the buyer (or imposing on the corporation in the case of a public share offering) guarantees regarding such matters as employment levels, notification regarding plant closures or the transfer of assets out of the country (or province), or subsequent resale. Contracts of performance containing such provisions are quite common in

France, but are notoriously unenforceable in less dirigiste economies. One should not assume, however, that the MOC option is free from the same pitfalls. Based on the cases examined in this chapter, there are little grounds for concluding that the reconciliation of divergent preferences for corporate behaviour is more easily achieved in the MOC than, say, through regulation or *ad hoc* agreements between the government and the corporation. And yet mixed ownership, save for circumstances where the state is providing equity that cannot be raised from private investors, or where the state shareholder is simply interested in a competitive return on its investment, implies that the state's ownership share may provide a lever of influence in the event of a serious difference in preferences for corporate behaviour.

The purpose of the decision-making analysis in this chapter is to determine the economic and political factors that have shaped the balance of influence between the state and private capital in the mixed ownership corporation. This is done through the examination of concrete instances of conflict in that relationship, demonstrating how state preferences have been expressed as attempted influence, what the reaction of private sector interests has been, and how these divergent expectations for the firm have been resolved. This approach to the decision process follows the work of Grassini on Italian state enterprise, Anastassopoulos on state companies in France, and Mazzolini on government-controlled corporations of Western Europe, in seeking to understand how corporate behaviour is shaped by the configuration of political and economic interests mobilized within and outside the organization.[2] Much of the evidence on which this analysis is based was collected through interviews with state and business principals who are or have been associated at some important stage with either Telesat, the CDC, or the Caisse.

The decision situations reviewed are the following:

1. Telesat Canada: i) the first (and subsequent) satellite acquisition by the corporation; ii) Telesat's application in 1976 to join the Trans-Canada Telephone System.

2. Canada Development Corporation: i) the federal government's request, in the autumn of 1980, that CDC management study Massey-Ferguson as a possible equity investment; ii) the federal government's attempt, in the spring of 1981, to replace the chairman of the CDC's board of directors with its own nominee.

3. Domtar Inc.: i) the 1981 takeover of Domtar Inc., by the Caisse and the Société générale de financement.
4. Canadian Pacific: the decision by the Caisse to seek representation on the board of directors of Canadian Pacific.

Based on a close examination of corporate operating histories, these decisions in which there was conflict stand out as crucial points in the determination of the relationship between the state or its agents and private capital in the mixed ownership corporation. At stake in each case was whether the firm would turn toward the state shareholder or toward management's own preferences. These conflicts involved such vital matters as major capital expenditures and financing (Telesat), investment behaviour and participation in corporate decision-making (CDC), and expanded state ownership and potentially control or at least state influence (Domtar and CP).

Examination of these several cases of decision-making in circumstances where the expectations of the state as shareholder (or, as the TCTS/Telesat case will demonstrate, some other part of the state with a relationship to the MOC) and its private sector ownership partners were divergent, indicates that the interests of this latter group are refracted through management's goal of maintaining corporate autonomy. Consequently the business/state relationship, as it unfolds within the MOC, is in fact a three-cornered relationship, involving the public and private shareholders and corporate managers. Variations in the pattern of the relationship will be determined by such factors as: (1) the set of private sector shareholders (ranging from widely-dispersed share ownership as in the case of the CDC, Domtar and CP, to relatively few private sector owners in the case of Telesat, the shares of which are not publicly traded); (2) the parts of the state with an interest in the decisions of the MOC, *and* the capacity to influence outcomes; (3) the sector of the economy in which the corporation operates, and the particular constraints on (and opportunities for) state intervention in this sector; and (4) the organizational structure of the mixed ownership corporation (i.e., the factors discussed in the previous chapter).

The focus on the resolution of conflict should not obscure the fact that the interests of the state as shareholder, and the private sector actors (shareholders, management, financiers), with which it is involved through the mixed ownership corporation, are frequently convergent. The chairman of the Caisse de dépôt, Jean Campeau, felt compelled to make this rather obvious observation in responding to the implicit criticism of the Caisse's equity investment activity which underlay Bill S-31. In Campeau's words:

> Bill S-31 alleges that since November 3 (1982), any share acquired by the Caisse or any share held or acquired exceeding the 10 per cent limit is acquired, not for profitability purposes, but for the purpose of sidetracking a company from its initial corporate goals for the benefit of Quebec. This is ridiculous. When one invests 200 million dollars in a corporation it would be ridiculous to think one does not seek profitability.[3]

If, however, the state's interest in its shareholdings was limited to the support of private capital accumulation or the expectation of a competitive return on invested capital, the question of how divergent expectations are reconciled in corporate decision-making would not arise. But as the examples of conflict reviewed will demonstrate, the state may have public policy goals considered by management and private sector shareholders to compromise the competitive performance of the corporation. Even where these goals are embedded within the charter of a mixed ownership corporation, as the objective of backward industrial linkages is set down, albeit ambiguously, in the *Telesat Act*, the state shareholder may find the corporation intractable as a policy instrument. Faced with a recalcitrant management, which generally is able to count on backing from the corporation's board of directors and the support of private sector shareholders, the state as principal shareholder is unable to impose its preferences over those held by management without precipitating a crisis of confidence that brings into question the viability of the mixed ownership capital structure.

The policy expectations that the state shareholder has for the mixed ownership corporation will be influenced by developments in the economic sector in which the corporation operates, and by the broader pattern of government policy. Thus, the Massey-Ferguson investment proposal which, *ex post*, became a source of tension in the relationship between the federal cabinet and CDC management, leading to the chairmanship crisis of May 1981, should be understood in the context of the crisis in the manufacturing sector of the Canadian economy symbolized by Massey-Ferguson's plight. The industrial strategy advocates within the Liberal Party dominated the government that was returned to power in 1980, and the general interventionism of this government combined with the acute crisis in central Canadian industry to prompt the CDC's principal shareholder to reassess its decade-old relationship as silent partner in the corporation's affairs. Similarly, the relocation of Domtar's Sifto division headquarters from Montreal to Toronto, and major capital expenditures by the corporation in Goderich, Ont., at a time when the Quebec government was intent on increasing salt mining within the province,[4] combined to convince the Quebec government that the 20 per cent ownership share held by the Caisse was not large enough to operate as a constraint on Domtar's investment decisions. (Certainly the decisions to relocate Sifto headquarters and expand the Goderich operation did not threaten the value of the Caisse's investment in Domtar. This is one factor that makes it implausible that the decision to acquire a controlling stake in the corporation did not originate with the Quebec government.)

The existence of private sector shareholders is a main limiting condition on state control of a publicly-traded corporation. Indeed, the 1981 confrontation between the CDC and the federal government over the chairmanship of the CDC provides a classic demonstration of how management is able to invoke its fiduciary responsibility to shareholders in resisting what it perceives to be the politically-motivated intrusions of the state as shareholder. In that particular case the support of the corporation's board of directors was instrumental in blocking an expanded government role in CDC decision-making. Similarly, the backing of the board of directors was a factor that reinforced Telesat management's position in resisting the federal government's preferences in the decision to acquire the ANIK A satellite (1970), and in bargaining for government compensation in the case of the ANIK D contract with SPAR (1979). Moreover, the limitation resulting from the fact of private sector shareholders (a structural condition) is compounded by a business ideology capable of accommodating direct investment by the state in the produce-for-profit economy, but which is extremely sceptical of the state as a partner in commercial decision-making. This ambivalence (a normative condition) is demonstrated in the attitudes of the Canadian business community toward the investment activities of the Caisse,[5] and is confirmed by the uniformly negative views expressed by management actors with the CDC and Telesat in regard to the workability of shared public/private decision-making.

Telesat Canada

(1) Satellite Acquisitions

All decisions concerning major capital expenditure decisions of Telesat involve the resolution of divergent expectations for this satellite communications corporation. On the one hand a Canadian content requirement is imposed upon Telesat by the terms of its charter, with the qualification that this will be "to the extent practicable and consistent with (the corporation's) commercial nature" (Section 5(2)). This rather ambiguous provision about Canadian content is reinforced by the statutory requirement that the corporation's capital expenditure proposals, whether for satellites or earth receiving stations, be submitted to the minister of communications for approval (Section 8). In this practice Telesat resembles a number of Western European mixed enterprises, including the French petroleum corporation, Société Nationale Elf-Aquitaine, in that the state investor is accorded a veto power over major capital decisions. On the other hand, alongside this expectation that Telesat will promote backward linkages, contributing to the development of a Canadian manufacturing capacity in satellite technology, is the statutory condition that Telesat be operated "on a commercial basis" (Section 5(1)), interpreted by the corporation's management as meaning profitable operation, and that in meeting the Canadian content requirements of the *Telesat Act* the commercial viability of the corporation will not be compromised.[6] Predictably, pressure for the utilization of Canadian suppliers, particularly SPAR Aerospace, has come exclusively from the government shareholder, while Telesat's management has insisted that the corporation be operated on a commercial basis.

The decision to select a United States supplier, Hughes Aircraft Company, for the first generation of Telesat satellites, over an RCA Ltd. proposal estimated to involve 65 per cent Canadian content (versus 20 per cent in the Hughes proposal, as finally agreed to), established a pattern in the relationship between Telesat management, the corporation's board of directors, and the government which has been maintained since. Directors and managers who were with Telesat at the time of this first satellite decision recall that the cabinet made clear its preference for the high Canadian content RCA proposal, but Telesat management resisted the policy signals coming from the government and entered a contract with Hughes at a per satellite cost which was half that of the RCA proposal.[7] The minister of communications, Eric Kierans, did not exercise his power of veto under Section 8 of the act and the only concession made to the government's interest in Canadian content was a negotiated increase in the value of work done by Canadian suppliers (i.e., Northern Electric and SPAR).

Telesat's ability to resist the nationalist preferences expressed by the government can be ascribed to a combination of factors. The corporation's management was determined that Telesat should be run as much like a private sector corporation as the terms of its charter and the government's 50 per cent ownership share would allow.[8] Autonomous corporate decision-making was therefore a necessary condition, and Telesat's first CEO, David Golden, was unrelenting in his insistence that the corporation's primary consideration had to be the provision of domestic satellite communications on a cost-competitive basis. In resisting the view that an equally important objective of the corporation involved the encouragement, through contracts, of a Canadian manufacturing capacity in satellite technology, Telesat management was able to invoke its corporate objects under the act. Because the charter is ambiguous about how far public policy goals (e.g., Canadian content) should intrude into corporate decision-making, the question of who determines this balance is crucial. In choosing Hughes as the supplier for the first generation of domestic satellites, Telesat management made the decision even though the government had maintained support for the high Canadian content RCA proposal,[9] and the Communications Research Centre of the Department of Communications had objected strongly to the idea that Telesat's satellite decisions should be independent of its own preferences for Canadian sourcing.[10]

In view of the divergent preferences of the government and Telesat management, the role of the corporation's board of directors became crucial. All seven members of this first board were appointees of the government, with three being drawn from the private sector, three from the public sector, and the seventh being Telesat's president, David Golden. Despite the government's expressed sympathy for high Canadian content, the directors were unanimous in supporting management's choice of the Hughes proposal. Such support was important in overcoming the government's reservations.[11] Had the minister of communications decided to exercise his veto under Section 8 of the act, in the face of the board's support for management's position, it would have been a clear signal to the government's ownership partners in Telesat (i.e., the common carriers), and to the CRTC (which would set the rates that Telesat could charge its customers), that the government considered the corporation to be primarily a public policy instrument rather than a commercial enterprise.

Since September 1970, when that first satellite decision was concluded, the proportion of Canadian content has increased regularly in subsequent generations of the ANIK satellite, reaching 50 per cent, with a Canadian prime contractor (SPAR

Aerospace) for the most recent ANIK D series of satellites.[12] This has not resulted from an increased sensitivity of Telesat management to the government's interest in backward linkages to the satellite industry. Rather, the explanation involves a combination of Canadian content premiums paid by the government to compensate Telesat for part of the higher cost of entering contracts with Canadian firms and, secondly, the development of a more competitive Canadian satellite industry (primarily SPAR Aerospace, which was nurtured through contracts from DOC and through its role as a subcontractor to Hughes in Telesat's ANIK A and ANIK C satellite procurements).

In having the cost of Canadian content isolated as a recompensable burden the corporation maintains the principle that the public policy interests of the government can be accommodated, but these interests do not form constraints that management needs to observe. The 1979 decision on the procurement of the ANIK D satellite demonstrates how the government's interest in the development of the Canadian satellite industry is taken into account by Telesat management. The government made it known that it favoured SPAR Aerospace as the supplier for this generation of satellites. This preference was not expressed through the DOC representatives on Telesat's board of directors, but through the deputy minister of communications, as is usual in negotiations between Telesat and the government over decisions concerning capital expenditure. The corporation's management contacted a number of suppliers for proposals, including the U.S.-based Hughes, which had been the prime contractor for the ANIK A and ANIK C satellites. The Hughes proposal was the most competitive, far lower than the price quoted by SPAR, but involved a low level of Canadian content. Telesat's president, David Golden, presented the government with the two proposals and said that Telesat would accept SPAR as the prime contractor on condition that Telesat be compensated for the difference in cost.

Thus, the preferences of the federal government were in conflict with those of Telesat management. When the subject of Golden's reappointment as president arose, as required each year under the terms of the *Telesat Act*, the board of directors was solidly in support of Golden's confirmation.[13] Whether the government was inclined to replace the president, as is its prerogative under the act is moot. But the board's implicit support for Golden's policy of treating the government's interest in Canadian content as a recompensable externality foreclosed this possibility unless, as had also been the case in the ANIK A decision, the government was prepared to force the issue of whether Telesat was foremost a commercial enterprise or a policy instrument.

(2) The Telesat/TCTS Membership Agreement

The agreement whereby Telesat became a member of the Trans-Canada Telephone System (since renamed Telecom Canada), a self-regulating consortium of common carriers in which Bell Canada is the dominant party, appeared to represent a step toward the government's expressed goal of an integrated terrestrial/satellite telecommunications system covering the entire area of Canada. The decision to seek membership in the TCTS originated, however, with Telesat management and was not related to this public policy objective.[14] While the federal government supported the Telesat/TCTS agreement, as demonstrated by cabinet's variance of the 1977 CRTC ruling, which proscribed the agreement as contrary to the public interest, the government's support was based on its acceptance of management's argument that the agreement was necessary to ensure Telesat a stable revenue base. It is highly improbable that the government was under any illusion that Telesat membership in the TCTS would provide it with a window on the telecommunications industry, allowing the government to participate directly in decisions regarding the national telephone system.[15]

The background to the Telesat/TCTS agreement is straightforward. In developing the original domestic satellite system, involving the three ANIK A satellites, Telesat management was responding to its mandate to put a system in place as soon as possible (dispatch was critical, given the international competition for limited geo-stationary satellite locations). Telesat was not building a system in response to demonstrated demand, and the market for the corporation's satellite channels, aside from anticipated contracts with the CBC and service to the remote North, was uncertain. Not surprisingly, a huge amount of excess capacity was built into this first system, with only eight full channels, out of the 36 available, leased to customers before the TCTS membership agreement. The weak income position of the corporation after becoming operational in January 1973 would have been worse had it not been for an unanticipated agreement between Telesat and RCA Global Communications/RCA Alaska Communications, whereby the latter leased a number of channels on an interim basis,[16] and a five-year contract with the Canadian Overseas Telecommunications Corporation (renamed Teleglobe), a Crown corporation that entered the agreement only under pressure from the government.[17] Indeed, the CBC and COTC together accounted for half of Telesat's regularly used channels during this early period in the corporation's operating history.

The obvious solution to this problem of soft markets was to acquire a share of the lucrative east/west long distance traffic. This market was dominated by the TCTS consortium, with CNCP Telecommunications occupying a comparatively minor position. Telesat management considered both the TCTS membership option and the alternative possibility of an integrated system with CNCP and Teleglobe.[18] The first option was judged most likely to provide Telesat with the income stability it considered necessary in view of the difficulties it had experienced in forecasting revenue.[19] Moreover, 10 of the 12 common carriers with equity in Telesat were members of the TCTS, so that the idea of Telesat operating in competition with the TCTS (as would have resulted from integration with CNCP) did not represent a real possibility without a major change in the corporation's ownership structure.[20] Under the terms of the agreement with the TCTS, Telesat undertook to respect the territorial markets of the respective TCTS members.[21] Most significant from Telesat's point of view was that the corporation would receive transfer payments from the TCTS, providing the income stability needed to finance the corporation's second generation of satellites. With neither the government nor the private banks prepared to finance Telesat's capital requirements,[22] and given that management was not inclined to press the government for new financing when Telesat was close to retiring an earlier government loan of $25 million, the agreement with the TCTS removed much of the uncertainty surrounding Telesat's income for future years while enabling the corporation to avoid financial dependence on the government.

The TCTS/Telesat membership agreement was disallowed by the CRTC as contrary to the public interest. In handing down this ruling the commission reasoned that integration of Telesat into the TCTS would make regulations of rates more difficult, a position that was supported by the Consumers' Association of Canada. Cabinet, which had previously approved the TCTS/Telesat agreement, overruled the commission's decision, so that it became apparent that the locus of state opposition to the idea of Telesat as a commercial enterprise was the CRTC and not the government as shareholder. Telesat principals maintain that the commission has construed from the fact of the government's 50 per cent ownership share that Telesat is a public service which happens to be run as a business, rather than a market-oriented telecommunications carrier which happens to have the government as a major shareholder.[23]

The circumstances of Telesat's entry into the TCTS demonstrate that the divergent expectations of the government as shareholder and those of the corporation's management, evident in the case of satellite procurement decisions, are not the only source of tension in Telesat's relationship to the state. Indeed, the corporation encounters the state in three separate guises. While the relationship with the Department of Communications is regular and generally carried out at a technical/cooperative level, the relationship between Telesat and the CRTC (the state as regulator) is regular and adversarial, and that between cabinet (the state as shareholder) and the corporation is episodic and frequently defensive. The particular case of Telesat's decision to join the TCTS involved a conflict between management's resolve that, with the second generation of satellites, Telesat should focus on commercial services and developing market opportunities, and the CRTC's concern with its ability to regulate rates and its understanding of Telesat as a public service organized as a business. In supporting Telesat management by varying the CRTC's ruling on the TCTS/Telesat agreement, cabinet appeared to have been acting on its interest in a domestic satellite system at the lowest cost to the government.[24] The situation demonstrated that the government's conception of the public policy objectives of Telesat was different from that held by the CRTC. Whereas the regulatory commission's concern was with competition in the telecommunications market and the rates charged to customers, the government's policy expectations for Telesat lay principally in the backward linkages that the corporation's capital expenditure decision could generate in Canada's satellite industry.

The Canada Development Corporation

(1) Massey-Ferguson

In the interminable debate over the need for a Canadian industrial strategy and the components of it (a debate that has been going on since at least the mid-1960s), the role of the CDC polarized the proponents of the two main rival views within the then governing Liberal Party and the senior federal bureaucracy.[25] This question of the CDC's relationship (or non-relationship) to the government's policy goals surfaced recurrently throughout the 1970s, dividing the more nationalist/interventionist members of the government from the less interventionist view centred in the Department of Finance,[26] with the latter view supported by CDC management and the business community. The tension between the CDC as a policy instrument (a view with which the prime minister was sympathetic) and the CDC as a holding company that just happened to be started with government seed money, but in which the government's ownership share would be reduced over time to 10 per cent (a view shared by CDC management, the then deputy minister of finance, Simon Reisman, and finance ministers Edgar Benson, John Turner, and Donald Macdonald, successively), existed during the first years of the CDC's operation. A pattern of non-intervention was established during this early period, which persisted until the return to office of the Liberals in 1980.

This pattern broke down in the period between CDC management's decision not to invest in the financially-struggling Massey-Ferguson corporation (autumn 1980), and the federal government's attempt to increase its leverage on the CDC board of directors (May 1981). The general interventionism of the Liberal government that was returned to power in 1980[27] (a government that, in the words of one very senior economic official, considered that it had been unfairly maligned by the business community in the late 1970s), the appointment of Allan MacEachen as minister of finance and Herb Gray as minister of Industry, Trade, and Commerce, two cabinet members known to be sympathetic to the industrial strategy concept,[28] and the rash of plant closings and the apparent decline of Canada's manufacturing sector were factors that brought about a reassessment at the cabinet level of the relationship of the CDC to the economic policies of the government.

This was the context in which the Massey-Ferguson investment issue arose. In fact, the question of whether the CDC should invest in the farm machinery corporation only became a political issue, understood as a subject of conflict, *ex post*. The decision by CDC management not to invest on strictly commercial grounds was considered by some members of the government, including the minister of finance, to be evidence of the insensitivity of the corporation to the interests of its major shareholder.[29]

The request that the CDC consider an investment in Massey-Ferguson was conveyed to the corporation's management by the deputy minister of finance, Dr. Ian Stewart. All the principals involved agree that no pressure was placed on the CDC. The corporation regularly received investment proposals from a wide range of sources, including MPs and officials in the federal bureaucracy.[30] The high level of the Massey-Ferguson proposal, issuing from the cabinet and conveyed through the deputy minister of finance, distinguished this particular case, as did the context of crisis in the central Canadian manufacturing sector that Massey-Ferguson's difficulties symbolized. CDC management's negative assessment of the investment was entirely predictable, however, because the corporation had previously studied (and rejected) the possibility of investing in Massey-Ferguson at the request of Conrad Black, chairman of the Argus Corporation.

Under finance ministers Turner, Macdonald, and Chrétien, the government had not been inclined to present the CDC with investment targets. An earlier proposal that the CDC invest in de Havilland which, along with Canadair, was purchased by the federal government in the mid-1970s, had come from Douglas Kendall. Kendall was chairman of de Havilland and a member of the CDC's board of directors. His proposal was made just after the Dash 7 had been certified, and de Havilland was optimistic about its commercial prospects. CDC management was less sanguine and rejected the investment as too risky. According to CDC officials, the federal government took no part in instigating the de Havilland proposal, nor did it apply any pressure even though IT&C clearly would have been pleased to see the CDC invest in the aerospace sector. The Massey-Ferguson proposal, which carried no suggestion of coercion, was consistent with this pattern of management autonomy in CDC decision-making. But the circumstances bearing on the CDC's relationship to the government had changed. The finance minister, Allan MacEachen, considered that the corporation should be more responsive to the public policy interests of its major shareholder, a view that was shared by the prime minister and other key ministers on the Priorities and Planning Committee of cabinet (notably Herb Gray and Marc Lalonde).[31]

Describing the circumstances of the Massey-Ferguson proposal, one CDC official observed:

> Massey was the only specific investment ever proposed to us by the government. The government had decided that it wanted Massey to survive, but it wondered about the practicality of its direct involvement in the corporation and saw the CDC as a source of management expertise.[32]

CDC management had several meetings with Massey-Ferguson's chairman, Victor Rice and, in the words of one official, the proposal generated a "lively internal debate in the CDC".[33] In the end it was decided that the costs of monitoring Massey's performance would be too high. The government did not offer the CDC any form of compensation as an inducement to invest in the farm machinery company. The *CDC Act* does not provide the authority for such an arrangement and, while admitting that an *ad hoc* payment was conceivable (for example, a management fee), one CDC official stated unequivocally that this would have been outside what the corporation found acceptable in its relationship with the government.

The CDC's rejection of the Massey-Ferguson investment proposal as commercially unsound raised to prominence the larger question of whether the government's 49 per cent ownership share should translate into influence over CDC investment decisions. The tradition of non-interference, which had developed through the 1970s, and the fact of private sector shareholders to whom CDC management could justifiably claim they owed a fiduciary responsibility, complicated the government's renewed interest in the corporation's possibilities as a policy instrument.[34] Insensitivity to government's policy signals, which CDC management had demonstrated in rejecting the Massey-Ferguson investment proposal, led to both increased tension between the corporation and its major shareholder, and recourse by the government to more coercive measures in attempting to enlarge its influence over CDC decision-making.

(2) The Control Crisis: 1981

In May 1981, the federal government tried unsuccessfully to replace the CDC's chairman, Frederick Sellers, with its own candidate, Maurice Strong. This failure must be understood in the context of the tensions generated by the CDC's refusal to invest in Massey-Ferguson, and a total breakdown in communication, including wilful misunderstanding, in the months preceding the control bid. The government was determined to increase its influence on the CDC's board of directors, but was stymied by a combination of factors, including: (1) the fact of private sector shareholders, a structural condition that served as a defence for management in resisting the idea that the CDC should pursue public policy objectives identified by the government; (2) the pattern of corporate autonomy that had been reinforced through successive investment decisions during the 1970s; and (3) the defensive hostility that had developed within the CDC, resulting from media reports of government dissatisfaction with the corporation after its failure to invest in Massey-Ferguson, without the government's views being communicated directly to CDC management.

CDC's rejection of the Massey-Ferguson investment proposal led to a reassessment by the government of the corporation's role and its relationship to public policy. The minister of finance considered that the CDC had become too isolated from its principal shareholder, and sought to increase the government's influence through new appointments to the board of directors.[35] According to a very senior state actor involved in the events leading up to the control crisis, an understanding was reached between the CDC and the minister whereby the government was entitled to nominate four new directors, and that these appointments could be made any time before the corporation's annual meeting in May 1981. Two of these nominations were made early in 1981, but the government waited until the week before the CDC's annual meeting before proposing its other nominees.[36]

In the interim, communications between the corporation and the government had broken down entirely. The chairman of the CDC, A. John Ellis, resigned in February 1981, and a new chairman, Frederick Sellers, was chosen without consultation with the corporation's major shareholder. Because of the strained relationship existing between the CDC and the government, this action could have been interpreted as a provocative demonstration of corporate autonomy. Notwithstanding the selection of Sellers, the government contacted a number of directors in April to express its preference for Maurice Strong as CDC chairman. With tensions aggravated by media reports of the government's desire to have Strong appointed to the chairmanship, the minister of finance proposed Joel Bell, then a vice-president of PetroCanada and well-known as an architect of the *Gray Report*, and David Beatty, a consultant with close connections to the Liberal Party, to fill the two directorships which the minister understood remained under the government's agreement with the CDC.[37]

The understanding, which state actors allege existed, broke down in the face of the particular nominations proposed by the minister of finance. CDC management considered Bell and Beatty to be too sympathetic to the policy instrument view of the CDC and refused to support their nominations. The government continued in its resolve to increase its influence on the board of directors, and the deputy minister of finance, Ian Stewart, met the board on the day of the CDC's annual meeting and restated his minister's case that Maurice Strong be named as chairman, and that Beatty and Bell be appointed as directors. As no one denies, the board was unanimous in opposing the minister's request. The government chose not to vote its equity on the issue.

At stake was whether the CDC's corporate autonomy would be infringed by recognizing the right of the major shareholder to significant voting representation on the board of directors. An increased government presence on the board was perceived by CDC management, the private sector directors, and the general investment community[38] as a compromise of the commercial orientation of the corporation. Strong and Bell were considered particularly objectionable because of their association with the development of PetroCanada.

The control crisis demonstrated to the government that its inability to control the CDC was structural, i.e., a function of the participation of private shareholders whose interests could be invoked by the corporation's management in opposing government influence.[39] Moreover, the particular resistance of CDC management to any intrusion upon corporate autonomy by its major shareholder reflected a view widely-held in the private sector, namely, that state decision-making involves considerations inappropriate to commercial activity. Between the structural constraint on the mixed ownership corporation as a policy instrument, and this normative bias against the state as a decision-maker in the produce-for-profit economy,[40] the government was confronted with the choice of effectively transforming the CDC into a state-controlled enterprise (through voting its equity and thereby precipitating a crisis that would certainly have resulted in the resignation of most board members and some of senior management, and a major decline in the market value of CDC shares) or conceding the intractability of the CDC as a policy instrument. In establishing the Canada Development Investment Corporation to eventually divest its interest in the CDC the government chose the latter course.[41]

(3) Qualifications to the CDC Case

While the focus of this chapter is on decisions in which there was conflict, it may be that the behaviour of a mixed ownership corporation (MOC) is shaped in subtle ways by the state's ownership participation. Or, it may be that the goals of management and private investors agree with those of the state shareholder, a fact that would not diminish the instrumental relationship of the corporation to public policy. In restricting the analysis to cases of conflict the reasoning has been that the resolution of divergent preferences is most likely to provide insight into the state's ability to pursue non-business values through the MOC. That coercion, compensation or retreat were the means by which the examined conflicts were resolved, should not be allowed to obscure the cooperative dimensions of business/state relations in the MOC. Some illustrations of this cooperative dimension surfaced during interviews with CDC actors. They suggest possibilities for the MOC to operate as an instrument of public policy when the state shareholder's preferences for corporate behaviour do not, in management's view, seriously undermine their own commercial goals for the firm.

The CDC's enabling legislation listed a number of Crown corporations as candidates for eventual acquisition. One senior executive who has been with the corporation from its inception said that this originally provided some guidance in delineating the areas in which the CDC would focus its investment activities (i.e., petrochemicals, oil and gas, and mining). But this official insists that particular investment decisions in these areas and the corporation's rapid expansion during its first 10 years of operation "were consequences of our own strategies," rather than being compelled by government pressure, the provisions of the *CDC Act*, or even the fact of state financial backing for the corporation.[42]

On occasion, this last element has been of some significance from the standpoint of lenders. Speaking of the $1.6 billion in debt financing for the 1981 acquisition of Elf-Aquitaine's Canadian assets, this CDC official suggested:

> The nature of the lender syndicate and the non-Canadian investment was different as a result of the guarantee that state involvement was perceived to carry.... Many of the European, Japanese and Asian investment houses do not have the sectoral expertise to judge their loans to the CDC but the government connection is something they find reassuring.[43]

Thus, the federal government's ownership participation has not hurt the corporation in raising debt capital, and may even have been of some marginal value in some acquisitions.

Two of these acquisitions warrant particular attention for what they reveal about decision-making free of conflict in the mixed ownership firm. The first is the CDC's 1973 acquisition of a 30.4 per cent share of Texasgulf. At the time of the acquisition all of the CDC equity was owned by t' e federal government. With neither an established earnings record nor a large cash flow to facilitate financing of the $271.4 million purchase, the corporation was relying on the federal government to subscribe for the full amount of equity provided for under Section 9 of the *CDC Act*.[44] In view of this dependence on the government, CDC management felt compelled to inform the minister of finance before the transaction was consummated. Moreover, because Texasgulf was an American corporation there was a possibility that the acquisition would have implications for Canada's bilateral relationship with the United States.[45] These two factors led management to notify the state shareholder of this pending transaction, a practice that was not followed once the corporation's financial independence from the government was established.

The second investment decision was the acquisition of the Canadian assets of France's Elf-Aquitaine in June 1981. CDC management had been trying to buy Elf since the summer of 1979. Company officials maintain that absolutely no consultation or exchange of information with the Departments of Finance and Energy, Mines and Resources, or any other part of the state, preceded this transaction. The introduction of the National Energy Program (NEP), which provided financial incentives for Canadian investors in the petroleum sector while excluding non-Canadian capital from the same benefits, did not change the relationship between the CDC and the government. The interaction between the corporation and Energy, Mines and Resources (EMR) in respect of Petroleum Incentive Payments and other aspects of the NEP was not different from the case of privately owned petroleum companies. Nonetheless, the NEP provisions favouring Canadian ownership made the timing right for the purchase of Elf, so in this case the government's goals for the petroleum sector and the CDC's goals for corporate growth dovetailed.

Some members of the Canadian petroleum industry, like Bob Blair of Nova Corporation and Jack Gallagher of Dome, publicly supported certain aspects of the NEP.[46] But despite being one of the largest Canadian companies in the petroleum sector, through its Canterra Energy holding, and benefiting from the provisions of the NEP, the CDC did not take a public position on the policy. In the words of one corporate official, "Given the government's status as a shareholder, we would have found a public position inappropriate".[47] Thus, even after establishing its financial independence from the federal government, CDC management appears to have been concerned that its autonomy not be cast in doubt. Support expressed publicly for the NEP could have suggested that the CDC was a policy instrument of the government, an image that management has always resisted.

(4) Domtar

During the first two weeks of August 1981, Quebec's Caisse de dépôt et placement increased its ownership share in Domtar from 25.5 per cent (July 31) to 41.4 per cent (August 11), thereby vesting effective control of this company with the Quebec state. This rapid takeover of Domtar appears to have been both congruent with the economic policy preferences of the PQ government, and to have involved unprecedented cooperation between at least two organizations of the Quebec state; the Société générale de financement (SGF) and the Caisse. The SGF borrowed $145.8 million in August 1981 to finance the purchase of 22 per cent of Domtar's equity, acquired mainly from the Caisse.[48]

A combination of two main factors led to the acquisition decision. In 1980 the Quebec government told SGF management that a controlling investment in a major corporation was desirable to stabilize the income base of this state holding company.[49] While other candidates for investment were studied, the Caisse's already large ownership stake in Domtar (approximately 20 per cent in the year before the takeover) was a factor that reduced the cost of acquiring control over this particular corporation, *assuming* that the combined ownership shares of the SGF and the Caisse can be taken to signify a single voice for purposes of control. The government's interest in seeing the SGF acquire a stable revenue base dovetailed with its interest in acquiring an effective veto, which could be used if circumstances warranted, over major capital and production decisions of Domtar. A series of decisions by Domtar management in the late 1970s, including the relocation of Sifto division headquarters from Montreal to Toronto, expansion of the capacity of its Goderich mine, and investment in a processing facility in Chicago to expand its share of the mid-American market, had demonstrated to the Quebec government that the Caisse's 20 per cent ownership stake was not sufficient to sensitize Domtar management to the economic development interests of the province.[50]

The effective takeover of Domtar by the Caisse and the SGF was brought about through the purchase of several small blocks of equity, rather than through a public takeover offer. This strategy was understandable from the joint perspective of the Caisse and the SGF. One state actor who was intimately involved in the takeover suggested that the public takeover option was estimated to cost $500 million, compared with the $300 million that the market purchase ultimately cost the Caisse and SGF.[51] However, the increase in the Caisse's ownership stake was later characterized by the Ontario Securities Commission as a takeover bid which, according to the act regulating securities trading in Ontario, requires a public offer to all shareholders.[52]

The reaction of Domtar's private sector shareholders, the corporation's financiers and the business community generally to the takeover was adverse. The market value of Domtar's common shares fell 15 per cent within a week of the news that the SGF and the Caisse together had acquired 42 per cent of Domtar's equity.[53] The suddenness and extent of this decline attested to shareholder uncertainty whether corporate autonomy could be maintained in the face of state control. The financial community had similar reservations, and these were communicated to senior officials of the SGF and the Caisse by a representative of the financial group which in the past had met Domtar's external capital requirements (in the words of one state actor, "I was submitted to the third degree, but in the end they were satisfied.").[54] The reaction of the business community was generally negative, and anxiety in the private sector over the future of Domtar and the possibility of other takeovers was not assuaged by the industry minister's statement that "there could be other Domtars," and Finance Minister Parizeau's acknowledgement that Paul Desmarais, chairman of Power Corporation, was instrumental in the takeover operation.[55]

Following the change in Domtar's ownership structure, the corporation's board of directors experienced considerable turnover in the two years after the takeover. But increased state representation on the board was not accompanied by any demonstrable attempts to impose public policy objectives on the corporation. Rather, the main effect of the state's controlling share, from the standpoint of decision-making, has been to sensitize management to the interests of its major shareholder. Thus, there is no evidence to suggest that Domtar's post-takeover decision to invest $773 million in a new manufacturing facility in Windsor, Que. was determined primarily by the industrial development preferences of the Quebec government. However, in deciding between alternative production possibilities and capital investments Domtar's management is cognizant of the latent power that its controlling shareholder might be able to wield in the event of a serious divergence between the preferences of management and those of the Quebec government. Domtar's president, James H. Smith, demonstrated his sensitivity to this constraint when he said: "One has to be conscious of the fact that a major block of the stock is controlled (by the Caisse and the SGF), but we've had no undue influence at all . . . . The government wants the company to be profitable." Smith added, "It might be different if we came to a decision to leave Quebec."[56]

In summary, the decision to acquire a controlling interest in Domtar was based on a combination of factors, including the government's interest in acquiring a veto over major capital and production decisions of one of the largest industrial employers in the province, the SGF's interest in stabilizing its income base, and that the Caisse's existing ownership share in Domtar rendered the cost of acquiring control lower than would have been the case with another corporation of comparable size.

The strategy followed in acquiring control over Domtar has been characterized as nationalization without public debate.[57] But the government's interest in controlling Domtar, through the ownership shares of the Caisse and the SGF, was not based on an expectation that the corporation would operate as an instrument of public policy. As a publicly-traded company Domtar's capital structure would be sensitive to any such intervention. Instead, it appears that the provincial government was concerned to sensitize the corporation's management to the general interests of its major shareholder, and thereby alter the relative weighting of the constraints on management decision-making.

(5) Canadian Pacific

The issues involved in the conflict between the Caisse and Canadian Pacific (CP) management over Caisse representation on CP's board of directors have been documented extensively.[58] CP management's categorical opposition to Caisse-nominated directors was a principal factor behind the introduction of Bill S-31 (*The Corporate Shareholding Limitation Act*), legislation that polarized the interests of the federal government and anglophone big business, on the one hand, against those of the Quebec state and much of the francophone business class on the other. Indeed, the limited issue of Caisse representation on the board of CP expanded to include the related question of the relationship between the Quebec government's economic policy and the investment decisions of the Caisse, as well as the more general question of whether and under what conditions state participation in private sector corporate decision-making, through representation on the board of directors, is acceptable to the business community.

To begin with the limited question of Caisse nominations to the board of directors of CP, the chairman of the Caisse, Jean Campeau, met Fred Burbidge, president and chairman of CP, in April 1982 and suggested that the Caisse be allowed to propose two nominees for appointment to the board of directors.[59] The

Caisse had acquired an additional 2 per cent of the equity of CP during the previous month, bringing its ownership share to roughly 9 per cent. In view of the wide dispersion of CP share ownership (Power Corporation, with approximately 11 per cent of equity, was the only other minority shareholder of significant size), a 9 per cent ownership share would carry under most circumstances a right of representation on the board of directors. This principle of proportional representation is consistent with the spirit of the *Canada Business Corporations Act*. CP's president immediately refused the Caisse's request, later citing uneasiness over the apparent public policy role of the Caisse, and its relationship to the economic development goals of the Quebec government, as the basis for his opposition.[60]

This rejection of the Caisse's request for representation was not an isolated case. The Caisse was refused representation on the board of directors of both Alcan and Dominion Textile, notwithstanding that in the latter corporation it had a greater ownership share than any other single shareholder.[61]

The private sector's aversion to direct state participation in corporate decision-making, so evident at the time of the federal government's loan guarantee to Chrysler[62] and, more recently, during Dome Petroleum's desperate efforts to avoid recourse to an equity bail-out by the federal government, is important in explaining these particular instances of opposition to Caisse representation on the board of directors. This general aversion is reinforced by the business community's perception that the investment orientation of the Caisse underwent a transformation with the departure of Michel Cazavan, formerly the Caisse's CEO, and his replacement by Jean Campeau. The elements that contributed to this perception are well known, and include: (1) the Caisse's 1979 decision to lend money to Hydro-Quebec and the Quebec government at rates of interest below the prevailing market rates (a policy that led to Eric Kierans' resignation from the Caisse's board of directors, on the grounds that the agency's fiduciary responsibility to its depositors was compromised); (2) the takeover of Domtar, in concert with the SGF; and (3) indications that the Caisse was following a systematic policy of increasing its equity holdings, and unprecedented statements suggesting that circumstances could compel the Caisse to intervene in the management of a corporation in which it held a large ownership stake.[63]

In opposing the Caisse's request for representation on CP's board, CP management was motivated by more than an aversion to the idea, and uncertain consequences, of shared control with a state agency. Management's concern with preventing *any* shareholder from acquiring a position of control over the corporation's decision-making (with control understood as the capacity to replace the corporation's top management) was demonstrated by the agreement between CP management and Paul Desmarais that placed a ceiling on the latter's ownership share.[64] CP management believed that the protection of corporate autonomy required the preservation of a widely held share distribution, a condition facilitating management dominance in corporate decision-making. While an accommodation with one of the leading members of Canada's corporate elite was conceivable, a similar *rapprochement* with the Caisse was excluded by the norms of corporate autonomy in the private sector and by the reservations held by the anglophone business class regarding the intentions of the Caisse and the relationship of that agency to the nationalist economic policies of the PQ government.

The decision of CP management to oppose Caisse representation on its board of directors was entirely consistent with a general pattern of private sector aversion to shared control with the state, which is evident in the results of a recent survey on the perceptions of chief executive officers regarding the Caisse (see Chapter 4). This aversion to Caisse participation in MOC decision-making, as opposed to investment *per se*, is not restricted to the anglophone business community, but is shared by francophone CEOs and even clients of the Caisse. The perception that the Caisse is not sufficiently insulated from influence by the Quebec government, reinforced by the particular circumstances of the Domtar takeover and CP management's resistance to the emergence of control blocks, were factors that combined to form the basis of CP's objection to Caisse representation.

Summary: Policy Instrument v. Corporate Autonomy

In the cases of conflicting preferences examined above, every *perceived* attempt by the state to influence corporate behaviour in a way considered prejudicial to the commercial competitiveness of the firm was opposed by management as an illegitimate intrusion into corporate decision-making. In a sense this merely demonstrates that the dynamic of capital accumulation, as it unfolds in a firm which relies on private investors for some part of its capital requirements, resists the imposition of politically-determined goals that reduce the competitive return on invested capital. The force of this limitation on state influence, however, seems not to have been appreciated by the governments which created Telesat, the CDC, and assigned both on equity investment and provincial economic development role to the Caisse. At least in the situations involving conflict over decisions examined in this study, original government expectations that the mixed ownership corporation would somehow operate as an instrument of public policy have in practice been stymied by management of the MOC, behind the protective shield of corporate autonomy.

In those cases where the state shareholder was successful in influencing corporate behaviour along lines opposed by management (i.e., greater Canadian content in Telesat's satellite procurements), or in changing the structure of decision-making (i.e., the takeover of Domtar), success came at a price. The practice of treating the federal government's preference for backward industrial linkages as a recompensable cost has protected the profit motive in Telesat's operations (though profitability has been elusive for other reasons). In other words, management has successfully opposed the view that the state's 50 per cent ownership share and privileged relationship to the corporation's decision-making structure should dilute corporate autonomy. Public policy is treated as an externality, the cost of which is borne by the state rather than the corporation. This is not an unreasonable attitude for managers to take and, as a number of CDC actors have suggested, it may even be a *necessary* attitude in view of their fiduciary responsibility to private shareholders. It appears that governments sometimes have been naive in their expectations for the MOC, not understanding the limits imposed by the MOC organizational structure, the fiduciary responsibility of management to private investors being one of these.

The alternative to inducement is coercion. But this option also carries costs, as the Caisse discovered after acquiring a controlling interest in Domtar. The immediate costs of the takeover (i.e., suspension of the Caisse from trading on the TSE, a drop in the value of Domtar's shares, temporary hostility on the board of directors and in the financial community) were small compared to the latent private sector hostility which eventually found expression in the Caisse/CP conflict and the controversy over Bill S-31. Thus, the price of forced compliance with the state shareholder's preferences may be crisis in the relationship between the state and private capital in the mixed ownership firm, a condition that was avoided in the CDC only when the federal government conceded defeat on the chairmanship issue.

These cases of conflict suggest that the reconciliation of divergent expectations of state and private sector for the MOC is likely to assume the form of a zero-sum game: a gain in state control corresponds to a reduction in corporate autonomy. The apparent inability of the state shareholder to substitute its own decision preferences for those of management and/or private investors, without either compensating the firm for the cost of carrying out these policy goals or precipitating a crisis in the relationship between the state and private capital, is a function of the specific circumstances of corporate organization examined in Chapter 2, and the configuration of political, business and organizational interests mobilized before a decision is made. Indeed, the cases examined in this chapter indicate a tendency toward the "spillover" of conflict, whereby the resolution of conflicting preferences for the firm is influenced by the broader pattern of business/ state relations in the particular sector of the economy in which the MOC operates.

As E.E. Schattschneider observes, conflict is contagious, and the resolution of what may have begun as a limited confrontation between distinct actors associated with the MOC will frequently be influenced by broader interests as the scope of conflict expands.[65] How the issue is defined will determine the scope and intensity of conflict between interests as, for example, the Caisse's decision to seek representation on the board of CP provoked two related controversies: (1) the relationship of Caisse action to the economic policy objectives of the Quebec government; and (2) the intergovernmental conflict between Quebec and Ottawa over spheres of authority in managing the economy.[66]

In the same way as the CP/Caisse conflict expanded to engage a broader range of actors and higher stakes, the confrontation between the federal government and the CDC over government influence on that corporation's board developed into a larger controversy which had been latent during the preceding years of non-interference by the government. The limited question of the CDC chairmanship and government representation on the corporation's board was transformed into the more fundamental issue of whether the CDC was, in any significant sense, a policy instrument. This issue had polarized opinion on the CDC from the mid-1960s, when the idea of a CDC first reached the public agenda. According to a senior economic official in the federal government, the division continued to surface periodically at the cabinet level throughout the 1970s.[67] What was at stake in this larger issue was the legitimacy of public policy preferences (particularly job maintenance and support for regionally and/or sectorally important firms) in the decision-making of a publicly-traded corporation. In other words, the outcome of a narrow decision (namely, the composition of

CDC's board of directors) was influenced by a larger controversy that had gone unresolved from the time of the CDC's creation.

In the case of Telesat, the issue of competition in Canada's telecommunications industry, i.e., whether the domestic satellite system should develop as a competitor with the TCTS (Telecom Canada), was resolved when the federal government varied the CRTC's rejection of the Telesat/TCTS membership agreement. But before this imposed settlement, the conflict between the CRTC and Telesat management had widened to set different factions of the telecommunications industry against one another, and ultimately placed the state as regulator (the CRTC) against the state as shareholder (cabinet). The specific matter of whether Telesat would be permitted to join the TCTS was transformed into the more general issue of the structure of competition in the telecommunications industry, with the further complication that different parts of the state held conflicting preferences for the satellite corporation's development.

Chapter 4

The Mixed Ownership Corporation as an Instrument of Public Policy: The Return on State Capital

The cases of conflict examined in the previous chapter are suggestive of the limits of the MOC as an instrument of public policy, when the expectations held by the state and management for the MOC are fundamentally at odds. Consequently, the view that retention of a state ownership share in a partially privatized state enterprise is sufficient guarantee of latent leverage over major decisions of the MOC receives little support from the experience of Telesat, the CDC and some of the private sector shareholdings of the Caisse. It would be absurd to suppose, however, that corporate behaviour that advances public policy goals of the state shareholder *necessarily* compromises the goals of managers and private investors. In order to assess the MOC as a policy instrument one needs to consider the overall coincidence between the state shareholder's expectations for its shareholding (or in the case of the Caisse, its shareholdings) and the actual performance of the MOC.

This is not simple. As John Langford observes:

> The recognition that the output of a public corporation – virtually by definition – contains some social benefits (or there would be no point in having it public) forces into the open the fact that public corporations almost inevitably have multiple goals. It is this phenomenon more than anything else which must be

> clarified in the discussion and measurement of efficiency and effectiveness.[1]

Conventional measures of commercial performance, such as profit, rate of return on invested capital, or some measurement of productivity, fail to tap the social benefits dimension to which Langford refers. To evaluate the non-commercial side of corporate performance whether for a wholly state-owned corporation or a MOC, one must identify the state investor's policy expectations for the firm.

These expectations may include profitability, so that public policy effectiveness and commercial effectiveness are not mutually exclusive. The direct investment record of the Caisse affords ample proof of this coexistence of profitability and the social returns which, Langford argues, are not measured by conventional standards of commercial performance. These social returns may involve such public policy goals as regional or sectoral economic development, reducing national dependence on foreign sources of supply for some commodity or, generally, goals that would not be pursued (or at least not to the same degree) by private capital because of the opportunity cost involved.

Moreover, the state shareholder's expectations for the MOC are not static. This was especially clear from examination of the conflict over government representation on the CDC's board of directors, an attempt at greater control which followed almost a decade of general neglect by the federal government. The circumstances that may lead to a change in a government's expectations for the MOC include developments in the sector in which the MOC is (or could be) involved, as well as changes in government and what might loosely be described as the ideological climate of state action. For example, the transition in 1985 from the PQ to the Liberal Party under Robert Bourassa in Quebec has been accompanied by plans for the *dénationalization* of some of the state investments acquired through the Caisse and the SGF, including the anticipated sale of the state's controlling share in Domtar. This issue of changing expectations is considered in the concluding chapter.

The conditions determining the public policy effectiveness of the MOC during the period covered by this study are not uniform across the three cases. Telesat, the CDC, and the private sector investments of the Caisse de dépôt et placement vary in terms of, *inter alia*, the combination of state and private sector actors, the sector(s) of economic activity, and state expectations for the corporation in which it holds an important ownership share. In the case of both the CDC and the equity holdings of the Caisse de dépôt, judgments have been passed by others on the effectiveness of these institutions as policy instruments. Less attention has been paid to Telesat because of the comparatively uncontroversial character of the corporation's purposes and decision-making, the smaller scale of its operations, and the fact that a *modus vivendi* between the state shareholder and its private sector equity partners was confirmed with Telesat's 1977 entry into the industry's vehicle for organizing unity among telecommunications carriers, the TCTS (now Telecom Canada).

From the standpoint of both their scale of operations and the issues raised by the partnership of private and public equity, the CDC and the Caisse holdings are incontestably of greater significance than Telesat. Moreover, the partial privatization of state assets, if carried out through a public share offering as has been typical of state divestitures in the U.K., West Germany and Italy, would result in MOCs in which the state would be a shareholder in publicly traded companies. Thus, the CDC model and the private sector shareholdings of the Caisse are much more relevant to the privatization debate than is Telesat with its closed capital structure. For these reasons the subsequent analysis of public policy effectiveness concentrates on the performance of the CDC and the Caisse group of companies, devoting only brief attention to Telesat.

Comparison of various objective measures of performance against the original and subsequent expectations held by the Quebec and federal governments for the Caisse's equity investments and the CDC respectively, provides a basis from which to assess the performance of these organizations as policy instruments. With regard to the subjective dimension of effectiveness, i.e., the degree of convergence/divergence in the expectations of the state and its private sector partners in the mixed ownership corporation, inferential measures are available for both the CDC and the Caisse. These include survey data on the perceptions held by private sector actors (shareholders in the case of the CDC; private sector CEOs for the Caisse, including the managers of corporations with a financial relationship to that state investment agency) regarding the relationship of the CDC and the Caisse's shareholdings to public policy.

Telesat

Though not a commercial success, Telesat represents a viable partnership of private and public capital, satisfying the federal government's goal of nurturing a high technology manufacturing capacity in satellites, management's goal of business-like operation (the main obstacle to which, according to Telesat officials, has been the rate decisions of the CRTC), and the industry's concern that the domestic satellite system not develop into a competitive threat to the heavily-capitalized terrestrial system. There is considerable truth in Doern and Brother's judgment that,

> Telesat Canada is a "holding" company, not in the traditional corporate sense of that word but in the political sense. It exists to secure a modicum of predictability among economic and political interests uncertain about exactly what to do about the future in a technologically complex field, but otherwise determined that if someone was going to lose from these developments, it would not be them.[2]

The fact that Telesat has been able to accommodate these various goals can be attributed to two main factors: (1) a limited set of shareholders (i.e., the federal government, the members of Telecom Canada, and CN/CP Telecommunications), each with clearly discernible interests in the corporation; and (2) the federal government's evident lack of concern that satellite communications develop in competition with the terrestrial system of east/west telecommunications. With the set of shareholders limited to the federal government and organizations in the telecommunications industry, none of whom maintains a stake in Telesat out of an expectation of a competitive return on their invested capital,[3] the corporation's decision-making is not complicated by the demands of the private equity market. Indeed, whatever pressures for competitive performance and expansion Telesat is subject to are generated internally, and represent management's own preferences for corporate development.[4]

With respect to the state shareholder's disinterest in Telesat as either an instrument for promoting competition in domestic telecommunications or extending federal control in a sector characterized by divided federal provincial jurisdiction,[5] one can only speculate as to how different Telesat's history would have been if the federal government had used the various levers of control available to it in order to pursue such goals.[6] The terrestrial carriers would certainly have withdrawn from Telesat under such a scenario, thus eliminating the mixed dimension of the corporation's ownership structure.[7] Precisely how the pattern of competition in telecommunications would have developed with a wholly state-owned satellite corporation, would have depended on the federal government's willingness to finance the capital costs of a more extensive satellite system and its readiness to subsidize the corporation's operating budget in the event that the user-cost of satellite communications was found to be uncompetitive with the terrestrial service.

If Telesat's actual performance is assessed against the federal government's goal, expressed through the DOC, of helping to develop a domestic manufacturing capacity in satellites, the corporation must be judged a qualified success. While the federal government is not called upon to subsidize the operating costs of the satellite company, the increasing proportion of Canadian content in Telesat's satellite acquisitions (ranging from approximately 20 per cent in ANIK A, to 30 per cent in ANIK B, 40 per cent in ANIK C, and finally 50 per cent in ANIK D) is directly attributable to the federal government's expressed preference for Canadian suppliers (particularly Spar Aerospace), and its willingness to subsidize the costs of economic nationalism. The contracts for the ANIK C and ANIK D satellite programs amounted to $53.6 million and $78.6 million respectively, for a total of $132.2 million. The federal government agreed to provide Canadian content premiums to a maximum of $26.6 million ($23.5 million of which had been paid out by the end of 1982) for these two series of satellites. This represents approximately 20 per cent of the total cost of these two satellite acquisitions, and close to 44 per cent of the value of all Canadian content (with the value of Canadian content calculated as approximately $21.4 million for ANIK C, and $39.3 million for ANIK D). In return for this considerable capital subsidy the federal government's goal of developing an indigenous manufacturing capacity in space communications has been furthered.[8]

This compensation principle allows for accommodation of the government's preferences while not compromising management's goal of business-like performance. As such, it represents the keystone in the *modus vivendi* agreed upon by management and the state shareholder. Pulling together the various threads of Telesat's performance, the corporation has joined private and public capital and business and public policy goals because of (1) the ability to isolate social cost as a recompensable expense, and (2) the fact that the corporation has not had to consider the reaction of the private equity market in accommodating the state shareholder's preferences. But Telesat's overall success as an MOC must be qualified by the observation that, despite several provisions of the corporation's charter which assign the federal government special privileges in corporate decision-making, and the fact that the federal government controls 50 per cent of Telesat's equity, the state shareholder's preferences have been experienced as pressure external to the corporation and its main purposes.

The CDC: 1971-1982[9]

The federal government's rather vague expectations for the CDC, until its 1981 defeat over the chairmanship of the corporation settled the future of the CDC as a private sector business, may be divided into three categories. In no order of precedence, these were:

(1) industrial policy expectations (the corporation would achieve diversity in its holdings, and industrial activities would comprise a significant share of the CDC's investment portfolio)[10]
(2) capital markets expectations (through its role as a wholly Canadian-owned investor, the CDC would contribute to increased Canadian control over economic decision-making in the *domestic* economy)
(3) government influence expectations (establishing the mixed ownership public company as a policy instrument)[11]

A fourth expectation held for the CDC by the government, the corporation's management and, from the time of the first public share offering, private sector investors, was that the corporation would operate at a profit. However, this was not, *ipso facto*, a public policy expectation, but rather a necessary condition for the CDC's acceptance by the private sector (and therefore its ability to raise equity capital on competitive terms). While the government never justified its investment in the CDC on the basis of anticipated income returns, the size of the public's financial stake in the corporation warrants evaluation of the CDC against this standard as well.

(1) Industrial Development

Considering first the corporation's contribution to diversified industrial development in Canada, it is fair to say that the CDC never outgrew the formative years during which it acquired Polymer (renamed Polysar), a 20 per cent interest in Petrosar, and a 30 per cent interest in Texasgulf. The Texasgulf acquisition was crucial in that it provided the CDC with a large regular base of earnings which enabled the corporation to establish its financial independence from the government. However, the overwhelming dominance of energy-related and mining investments in the corporation's balance of assets was reinforced over time. This is demonstrated by the following figures.

TABLE 4.1
CDC assets by industry segment*

	($ millions)	(%)		
Oil and gas	2,918.4	38.8	69.0	87.8
Petrochemicals	2,271.8	30.2		
Mining	1,415.3	18.8		
Office information products	689.5	9.2	11.6	
Industrial automation	38.7	.5		
Life sciences	108.6	1.4		
Venture and expansion capital	38.8	.5		
Fisheries	24.6	.3		
CDC Corporate	20.2	.3		
Total	7,525.9	100.0		

REVENUE DISTRIBUTION*

	($ millions)	(%)		
Oil and gas	567.0	14.0	68.1	76.1
Petrochemicals	2,168.2	54.1		
Mining	322.1	8.0		
Office information products	636.2	16.9	21.2	
Industrial automation	30.2	0.8		
Life Sciences	139.5	3.5		
Interest and other income	148.1	3.7		
Total	4,011.3	100.0		

CONTRIBUTION TO NET INCOME*

	($ millions)	(% of net income loss)	
Oil and gas	-14.4	42.1	71.8
Petrochemicals	-38.6		
Mining	-37.3		
Office information products	-10.3	9.7	
Industrial automation	- 5.8		
Life Sciences	3.9		
Venture and expansion capital			
Fisheries	- 7.1		
CDC Corporate	-16.2		
Net Income	-125.8		

*Note: As of December 31, 1982.

Source: Canada Development Corporation, *Annual Report*. 1982.

The CDC's assets picture during the period when it could have been considered a policy instrument was dominated by energy-related investments. Including mining activities, the natural resource extraction and processing component of the corporation accounted for 87.8 per cent of total assets in 1982. By comparison, the manufacturing/high technology segment of CDC investments, comprising office information products, industrial automation systems, life sciences and venture capital, constituted 11.8 per cent of the corporation's assets. In view of the preponderance of energy-related and mining activities, it must be questioned whether the corporation made the contribution to diversified industrial development in Canada that was expected of it.

During the decade leading up to the major confrontation between the CDC and the federal government, the corporation rejected numerous investment proposals coming from MPs, business organizations and federal bureaucrats (though, significantly, not from cabinet until the Massey-Ferguson proposal).[11] They were rejected on the grounds that they did not satisfy the sectoral and commercial objectives that management had established for the firm and that in management's view they typically reflected a misconceived notion that the CDC was somehow different from other investment holding companies by virtue of the government's involvement. In evaluating the corporation's contribution to *diversified* industrial development one should keep in mind that the CDC was debated and created during a period when Canada's weak manufacturing/technology base was an important policy issue, linked in the minds of many (including the authors of the *Gray Report*) to the level of foreign ownership in the Canadian economy. Even though the Liberal government appears to have been confused in its goals when it was creating the CDC, it would still seem unreasonable to suggest that all Ottawa intended when it invested a quarter of a billion dollars in the firm was to subsidize the industrial status quo.

When the CDC's investments are broken down by location, one finds that at the time of the crisis in the corporation's relationship to the federal government (the period between autumn 1980 and the annual shareholders' meeting in May 1981) a significant proportion of both the CDC's assets and income was generated by non-Canadian holdings. The fact of considerable overseas holdings is relevant in two respects: (1) the profitable operation of foreign subsidiaries makes a positive contribution to Canada's balance of trade, through the surplus value generated abroad and transferred to Canada in the form of dividends;[12] and (2) investment in productive activity located outside Canada does not contribute to industrial development of the domestic economy. The extent of the CDC's non-Canadian operations is demonstrated by the figures in Table 4.2.

At the time of the crisis in the relationship between the CDC and its major shareholder, roughly 30 per cent of the corporation's assets were located outside Canada (principally in the United States and the EEC), accounting for approximately 40 per cent of revenue and a quarter of the CDC's operating profit in 1980.[13] While the balance between domestic and foreign operations changed dramatically in 1981, due to the purchase of Aquitaine Company of Canada Limited from France's Société Nationale Elf-Aquitaine, and the acquisition of Texasgulf's Canadian assets, this shift was not a consequence of a deliberate policy to retrench the corporation's foreign operations. In fact, the real value of the corporation's assets in the United States increased between 1980 and 1981 and remained constant in Europe. Provisions of the NEP favouring Canadian ownership were the key factor in the timing of the Aquitaine acquisition, an investment that doubled the size of the CDC's asset base.

A survey of the CDC's major acquisitions between the corporation's creation and the defeat of the federal government in 1981 over the control issue, demonstrates the indifferent contribution which the CDC made during this period to industrial development in Canada. (See Table 4.3.) Only two of these major investments, Petrosar and Allelix, involved the generation of new productive capacity. All of the other transactions represented a transfer of ownership in existing assets.

(2) Increased Canadian Ownership

In expanding Canadian ownership of the domestic economy, Texasgulf, Tenneco, and AES Data represent the three cases where CDC investment displaced foreign capital in the Canadian economy (the 1981 acquisitions were consummated after management's successful assertion of independence from the federal government). Polysar, Connaught Laboratories, and Fishery Products involved the transfer of equity from Canadian owners (the Crown in the case of Polysar) to the CDC, while A/S Dumex was based in Denmark with subsidiaries in several other countries. Therefore, from a *qualitative* standpoint the CDC's performance in patriating important production assets has been mixed. The corporation's 1973 investment in Texasgulf, and the 1975 acquisition of the Canadian assets of Tenneco, are the two cases most frequently cited as evidence that the CDC satisfied the

TABLE 4.2
CDC Assets, Revenue, and Operating Profit by Geographic Division (in millions of dollars)

	Canada	United States	Europe & rest of world	Eliminations*	Total
Assets					
1980	1,793.6 (73.4%)	254.3 (10.4%)	480.4 (19.7%)	[85.0] (3.5%)	2,443.3
1981	5,535.2 (83.8%)	664.2 (10.1%)	527.4 (8%)	[121.8] (1.8%)	6,605.0
1982	6,048.5 (83%)	1,027.4 (14.1%)	378.1 (5.2%)	[168.4] (2.3%)	7,285.6
1983	6,104.1 (83.2%)	937.3 (12.8%)	310.0 (4.2%)	[10.5] (0.1%)	7,340.9
Revenue					
1980	1,523.6 (64.6%)	362.2 (15.4%)	761.5 (32.3%)	[341.6] (14.5%)	2,359.2
1981	2,173.0 (69.3%)	522.4 (16.7%)	740.7 (23.6%)	[386.4] (12.5%)	3,136.4
1982	2,419.5 (61.2%)	993.2 (25.1%)	736.6 (18.6%)	[344.1] (8.7%)	3,953.3
1983	2,092.2 (54.6%)	1,266.3 (33.0%)	752.4 (19.6%)	[385.3] (10.0%)	3,834.7
Operating Profit					
1980	194.4 (75.6%)	6.7 (2.6%)	60.8 (23.7%)	[4.9] (1.9%)	257.0
1981	227.9 (83.0%)	10.1 (3.7%)	34.7 (12.6%)	[1.8] (0.7%)	274.5
1982	166.3 (80.3%)	7.2 (3.5%)	32.9 (15.9%)	[0.8] (0.4%)	207.2
1983	119.1 (48.9%)	8.4 (3.4%)	115.6 (47.5%)	[0.4] (0.2%)	243.5

* The eliminations category represents inter-corporate transfers between CDC holdings.

Source: Canada Development Corporation, Annual Report, 1981, 1982, 1983.

TABLE 4.3
Major CDC Investments

Year	Acquisition
1972	Polysar ($72 million)
1972	Connaught Laboratories ($24 million)
1973	Texasgulf (30.4% at a cost of $271.4 million) 1973 Petrosar (51% interest at a cost of $25 million, through Polysar) 1973 A/S Dumex (75% interest at a cost of $11.1 million)
1975	CDC Oil & Gas Limited (the Canadian assets of Tenneco Inc., for $110.8 million)
1975-76	Petrosar (20% direct interest at a cost of $9.9 million)
1978	AES Data Ltd. and Wordplex Corporation (initial payment of $28.1 million)
1980	Fishery Products Ltd. (40.8% interest at a cost of $34.4 million)
1980-81	Allelix (50% interest, along with John Labatt Ltd., and the Government of Ontario, in this biotechnology company)
1981*	Aquitaine Company of Canada Ltd. (from SNEA for $1.6 billion)
1981*	Canadian assets of Texasgulf (in exchange for the CDC's 35% interest in that corporation, and $536.7 million)
1981*	Sentrol Systems Ltd. (85% interest at a cost of $20.9 million)
1981-82*	Savin Corporation (New York) (57% interest at a cost of $75 million)

* The acquisition occurred after the control crisis.

Source: Canada Development Corporation, *Annual Report*, 1972-1982 (various years).

federal government's expectation that it contribute to domestic ownership in sectors of the economy characterized by a low level of Canadian equity. But CDC management insists that in each case the Canadianization objective was incidental, given that CDC management had identified (1) petroleum and natural gas, and (2) mining, smelting, and refining, as two areas in which to concentrate the corporation's investment activity.[14] The principal factor in choosing Texasgulf in 1973 and Tenneco in 1975, rather than two other corporations, was the feasibility of acquiring control in each case.

If there was nothing in particular about the CDC's balance of investment activities to suggest that it operated as an instrument of public policy, one might at least have expected that the corporation's shareholder population would differ from its wholly private enterprise counterparts. This expectation is based on the government's argument that a Canada Development Corporation would constitute "people's capitalism," providing ordinary citizens with an opportunity to invest directly in Canada's economic development. But the government was thwarted by the opposition of investment dealers to the marketing of shares through the chartered banks. In consequence, the CDC's first public offering of shares in the autumn of 1975 was handled entirely by investment dealers, thereby imposing the usual limitations on the range of people likely to be aware of and disposed to purchase the share offering. By contrast, the first public offering of shares in the British Columbia Resources Investment Corporation (BCRIC), in May and June 1979, was marketed through a range of financial institutions comprising the banks, trust companies, credit unions, and investment dealerships. The distribution of sales in the BCRIC case demonstrated the crucial role of the more "democratic" intermediaries in providing access to a wider investing public. Seventy-one per cent of BCRIC's shares were sold through banks, credit unions and trust companies. Altogether, just under 170,000 Canadians of British Columbia residence purchased shares. In comparison, the initial issue of CDC shares was bought by approximately 20,000 Canadian investors.

In relation to such characteristics of the CDC shareholding population as geographic location, annual income, investment holdings, and socio-economic status, the corporation's shareholders were typical of that stratum of the population which invests directly in corporation stock.[15] Most revealing was the investment holdings profile of CDC shareholders. The CDC did not succeed in attracting the savings of Canadians who typically would not be given to direct equity investment. In fact, 80 per cent of CDC shareholders were holders of common shares in other companies, with an equal proportion owning preferred shares of one or more corporations. This compared with a figure of under 10 per cent for the population as a whole.

TABLE 4.4
Investment Holdings of Original CDC Shareholders

Size of Portfolio*	Number of Shareholders	Percentage of Shareholders	
Under $2,500	412	9.5	
$2,500 - 5,000	392	9.0	
$5,000 - 10,000	530	12.2	
$10,000 - 15,000	416	9.6	
$15,000 - 20,000	340	7.8	
$20,000 - 30,000	407	9.4	52.1
$30,000 - 50,000	521	12.0	
Over $50,000	1,334	30.7	
No response	114	-	
Total	4,466	100.0	

*Excludes tangible property like real estate and businesses.
Adapted from Dr. R.F. Kelly, *Shareholder Survey* (Vancouver, 1976).

(3) The Mixed Ownership Public Company as a Policy Instrument

Because of its ambiguous organizational structure, the CDC was from the beginning concerned with how the public, and particularly the investment community, perceived the relationship between the CDC and government. Management's recognition of the sensitivity in the relationship between market value of CDC shares and perceptions regarding the likelihood of government intervention in the management of the corporation, resulted in regular avowals of corporate autonomy, and periodic assurances from the government (usually timed to coincide with a public share offering) that it would refrain from participation in the affairs of the CDC. Despite regular attempts to clarify the role of the CDC and its relationship, or non-relationship, to public policy, confusion persisted. A survey of the CDC's original shareholders showed that this uncertainty was not restricted to the general population.

Evidently, the CDC was not entirely successful in laying to rest the perception that it was intended to be an instrument for the repatriation of economic decision-making. Only 30 per cent of the responding shareholders disagreed with the suggestion that the CDC was intended to play a Canadianizing role, and 60 per cent considered that the corporation was somehow different from other financial institutions. At the same time a majority of respondents listed "Safe Investment" as either their first or second reason (from a list of nine alternative reasons) for investing in the CDC , a greater proportion than for any other investment rationale. The fact of widespread confidence in the soundness of the CDC as an investment, coincident with (1) shareholder division over whether the CDC was intended to play

TABLE 4.5
Shareholders' Perceptions Concerning the CDC

Statements concerning the CDC	Agree	Neither agree nor disagree	Disagree
The CDC is designed to buy back Canada from foreign investors.	40.7	29.3	30.0
The CDC is no different than any other financial institution.	16.7	23.2	60.1

Adapted from Dr. R. Kelly, *Shareholder Survey* (Vancouver,1976).

a Canadianizing role, and (2) general agreement with the proposition that the CDC was somehow different from other financial institutions, is explained by two facts attendant upon the 1975 public share offering. First, the government's public assurance that it would not be involved in the management of the corporation featured prominently in the share marketing. Second, and probably of greater significance, were the generous terms of the equity issue itself. These included a competitive dividend yield, buy-back and bonus share provisions, and an instalment purchase plan. These conditions were enough to offset any uncertainty regarding the relationship between the corporation and the government.

Clearly, the concept and practice of the mixed ownership public company as an instrument for joint public sector/private sector decision-making in the economy was not advanced by the experience of federal government participation in the CDC. This is confirmed both by the private sector's ambivalence toward the CDC, evident from the 1976 shareholder survey and the stock market's negative reaction to the government's 1981 influence attempt, and by an examination of CDC decision-making. The analysis in the previous chapter concluded that by the time the government's vague expectations of influence congealed into concrete attempts to determine particular outcomes, the possibility of transforming the corporation into a policy instrument was ruled out by a structural condition (i.e., the existence of minority shareholders and their rights under the *Canadian Business Corporations Act*) and by years of non-participation by the state shareholder in corporate decision-making, which enabled management to consolidate its position of effective control.

(4) Income Returns on the Public's Investment

There remains the test of the CDC as an *actionnariat de l'état*. On this count the corporation was a failure, as the government actually lost money on its investment in the CDC. Before the 1985 divestiture of all but 10 per cent of its interest in the CDC the federal government held approximately 47 per cent of the corporation's equity, all of this in the form of common shares (the federal government held about 83 per cent of all shares in this category). The government never received dividend income from its equity. The 53 per cent of private equity was concentrated in the preferred share classes, yielding regular annual dividends. In the absence of dividend payments the government's only means of receiving an income return from its investment was through divestiture. The partial divestiture that took place in 1985-1986, when the government sold over three-quarters of its equity, raised $254 million. This must be considered against the fact of an initial government investment of $250 million, in 1971 dollars.

One additional aspect of this financial question must be considered. This involves the transfer in 1972 of Polymer Corporation Limited, previously a Crown corporation, to the CDC in exchange for $72 million worth of common shares. Whether this represented the true market value of Polymer is moot, but it is worth noting that some financial analysts believed this was an unrealistically low transfer price. But even if one assumes that the Canadian public received fair value in what amounted to the privatization of a Crown corporation, future income was lost through the transfer of Polymer (renamed Polysar), a commercially successful operation throughout most of its history. The present and future value of the corporation, as realizable through dividend payments and/or appreciation in the market valuation of Polysar's operations, was lost to the general public (in exchange for $72 million of CDC shares which never paid a dividend, and which in real terms depreciated over time) and acquired by an incomparably smaller segment of the population that benefited through the contribution made by Polysar to the CDC's profitability.[16] Understood from the standpoint of opportunity cost, the transfer of Polymer represented a loss to taxpayers, not less real for its difficulty of precise measurement.

The Caisse Shareholdings

Examination of the Caisse's origins and subsequent assessments of its role reveal a broad area in which the Caisse is free, within the limits imposed by management's fiduciary responsibility, to invest directly in private sector corporations with an eye to provincial economic development. While the Caisse is not precluded from direct investment in corporations without significant Quebec operations (nor even from investing in non-Canadian equity, although there is a 10 per cent ceiling on the proportion of a pension fund's assets which may be invested in foreign securities), there has always been a clear expectation that "Quebec" corporations would receive priority.

In relation to equity investment and the province's economic development, three expectations have remained constant since creation of the Caisse was advocated in the early 1960s by the *Conseil d'orientation économique du Québec* and the Dupont Commission. These expectations are that:

1. The Caisse will invest some portion of its capital in the bonds and shares of Quebec-based corporations, so that savings generated in the province contribute to expansion of the indigenous economy.

2. Assuming sound income prospects, the Caisse will participate in financing projects initiated by some other part of the state or by the private sector.

3. Through its size and interventions in the province's capital markets, the Caisse will acquire a position of moral authority, allowing for suasion instead of coercion, in the private sector of the Quebec economy.

Performance against the first two expectations can be measured using financial information. The third expectation is properly understood as the legitimacy that the private sector accords the Caisse as an investor. This subjective condition is assessed with the use of inferential data, primarily the results of a recent survey regarding CEOs' perception of the Caisse.

(1) Investing in the Quebec Economy

In 1967 the Caisse began to invest in the shares of private sector corporations. Since then, equities have accounted for between 11.4 per cent (1967) and 23.1 per cent (1984) of the agency's total investments, while the dollar value of this portion of the Caisse's portfolio has increased from CAN$47,551,487 (1967) to the current value of just over $5 billion (1985). Corporation bonds constitute another area of private sector investment by the Caisse. While the purchase of debt instruments does not carry ownership prerogatives, corporate bond issues are generally used to finance capital projects, and therefore an investment in bonds frequently will contribute more directly to economic development than would the purchase of a corporation's shares. Corporation bonds comprised an important part of the Caisse's investment portfolio until the late 1970s, but over the past several years they have accounted for a declining share of total investments, and the absolute value of the Caisse's private sector debt assets has fallen dramatically. The pattern of change over time is demonstrated in Table 4.6.

Since 1982 the Caisse has published in its annual report a list of the private sector corporations in which the agency has investments, in the form of shares and/or bonds. This information enables one to measure the extent to which the Caisse, through its investment behaviour, contributes to the financing of Quebec-based corporations. The operational definition of a Quebec-based corporation, as used here,[17] has two components: (1) majority control is held by residents of Quebec; and (2) the corporation's head office is located in the province.[18]

TABLE 4.6
The Caisse's Investment in Corporation Bonds and Shares (In Millions of Dollars, and as a Percentage of Total Investment)

Year	Shares		Bonds		Total Investments
1985	$5,024.8	(22.8%)	$378.2	(1.7%)	$22,068
1984	4,570.4	(23.1%)	368.6	(1.9%)	19,745
1983	3,563.6	(20.0%)	519.7	(2.9%)	17,851
1982	2,759.6	(17.3%)	746.6	(4.7%)	15,906
1981	2,316.7	(17.0%)	887.4	(6.5%)	13,639
1980	1,496.4	(13.0%)	964.3	(8.4%)	11,508
1979	1,105.7	(11.6%)	945.3	(9.9%)	9,555
1978	920.1	(11.8%)	677.8	(8.7%)	7,826
1977	841.4	(13.4%)	593.2	(9.4%)	6,288
1976	823.8	(15.8%)	534.5	(10.2%)	5,224
1975	721.5	(17.2%)	430.2	(10.2%)	4,230
1974	656.1	(18.8%)	361.6	(10.3%)	3,499
1973	518.6	(17.9%)	290.6	(10.0%)	2,901
1972	371.9	(16.9%)	264.0	(12.0%)	2,206
1971	295.2	(16.9%)	204.3	(11.7%)	1,743
1970	224.8	(16.5%)	108.0	(7.9%)	1,365
1969	156.6	(15.8%)	45.6	(4.6%)	990
1968	99.2	(14.5%)	37.6	(5.5%)	684
1967	47.6	(11.3%)	21.4	(5.1%)	418
1966	--		0.3	(0.2%)	183

Source: Caisse de dépôt et placement, *Annual Report*, 1966-1985.

Examination of the Caisse's equity portfolio as of December 31, 1985,[19] reveals that less than 20 per cent of the Caisse's total investment in corporate shares was accounted for by Quebec-based corporations. Shares in Domtar, Vidéotron and Provigo together account for 5.7 per cent of the total value of the Caisse's equity portfolio, and approximately a third of the dollar value of all shares held in the Quebec-based corporations listed in the Caisse's annual report. In the case of corporate bonds, Quebec-based businesses constitute about 21 per cent of the value of those investments listed in the Caisse's 1985 breakdown. This should be viewed against 22 per cent of these aggregated investments being accounted for by the bonds of Bell Canada Enterprises, Campeau Corporation and Interprovincial Pipelines, three corporations that are not based in Quebec. These figures are summarized in Table 4.7.

Review of the Caisse's shareholdings reveals that 92 per cent of the market value of the agency's equity portfolio is accounted for by shares held in 29 corporations, only three of which, Provigo, Vidéotron, and Brascade, generate the major part of corporate income from operations in Quebec. Brascade represents a partnership between the Caisse and Toronto capital (notably the Bronfman family which, through Brascan Ltd., controls 70 per cent of Brascade) and does not satisfy the requirements of a Quebec-based corporation, as defined earlier. (See Table 4.8).

The predominance of blue chip stocks in the Caisse's equity portfolio demonstrates that a competitive return on investment is the principal consideration determining the Caisse's direct investment behaviour. It was this phenomenon of heavy investment in the shares of non-Quebec corporations that led Pierre Fournier, a prominent Québécois political scientist, to argue that the Caisse had contributed to the "haemorrhage" of Quebec savings.[20] But in fact the size of the Quebec equity market represents a main limitation on the Caisse's purchase of shares in Quebec-based corporations. This was remarked upon several years ago by Marcel Cazavan, former president of the Caisse:

> With regard to shares, Québec corporations certainly are favoured. But the extent of the Caisse's purchases renders it impossible that these investments can be limited to Quebec without taking up everything that is issued. This would mean that the Caisse would take control of all Quebec corporations, which is neither allowed nor desirable.[21]

TABLE 4.7
Major Caisse Investments in Quebec-based Corporations*
(December 31, 1985: in thousands of Canadian dollars)

Corporation	Value of shares held by the Caisse	Value of bonds held by the Caisse
Artopax International	4,484	--
Banque Nationale du Canada	62,577	11,687
Comterm	5,144	--
Caisse Centrale Desjardins	--	20,086
Consolidated-Bathurst	27,699	--
Coopérative Fédérée	--	6,641
Crédit Industrial Desjardins	--	8,746
Domtar	138,997	--
Donohue	7,246	8,518
Fédération des Caisses populaires Desjardins du Québec	--	5,154
Gaz Métropolitain	21,138	6,222
Ivaco	25,322	--
Logistec	1,415	--
Marine Industries	126	7,377
Noranda Wines	44,878	--
Peerless Tapis	--	7,552
Place Desjardins	--	8,426
Power Corporation	155,000	--
Prenor Group	8,832	--
Provigo	70,740	203
Reitman's (Canada)	18,582	--
Société d'investissement Desjardins	14,185	--
Steinberg	47,572	--
Télé-Metropole	13,018	--
Trust Général	20,427	5,050
Vidéotron	74,464	2,980
Sub-total	761,846	98,642
Total investment in each category	5,024,800	378,200

* Note: These investments comprise all Quebec-based corporations in which the market value of the Caisse's holding exceeds $5 million, together with those enterprises in which the Caisse holds at least 10 per cent of voting rights.

Source: Caisse de dépôt et placement, *Rapport de gestion*, 1985 (tableau 13).

TABLE 4.8
Caisse Shareholdings Valued at $50 Million or More

	As of December 31, 1985 (millions of dollars)	As of December 31, 1982 (millions of dollars)
Canadian Pacific	543.2	255
Bell Canada Enterprises	454.8	104
Alcan	342.1	217
Toronto-Dominion Bank	247.5	69
Seagram	233.6	109
Royal Bank	231.4	164
Imperial Oil	219.1	84
Moore Corporation	198.4	50
Northern Telecom	188.5	64
Hiram Walker Resource	164.3	74
Brascade Holdings	161.5	179
Power Corporation	155.0	--
Domtar	139.0	88
Bank of Montreal	136.7	77
Bank of Nova Scotia	135.5	143
Thomson Newspapers	127.9	29
TransCanada Pipelines	107.5	29
Dofasco	101.7	25
Genstar	89.3	13
John Labatt	84.0	41
Vidéotron	74.5	7.3
Provigo	70.7	69
Nova	69.0	77.7
Placer Development	66.6	13.5
TransAlta Utilities	64.5	--
National Bank of Canada	62.6	19.7
Norcen	59.1	48.9
PanCanadian Petroleum	59.0	32.9
Canadian Imperial Bank of Commerce	58.7	66

Source: Caisse de dépôt et placement du Québec, *Rapport de gestion*, 1982, 1985.

As of 1983, only 39 of the 175 largest Quebec-based corporations (a category that included state enterprises) were publicly traded on one or more Canadian stock exchanges. There remain, therefore, important limits on the set of provincially-focused enterprises in which the Caisse may invest directly. As for investment in non-Quebec corporations with substantial operations in the province, the federal government's introduction in 1982 of *The Corporate Shareholding Limitation Act*, legislation that proposed to restrict the capacity of provincial governments and their agents to invest in corporations with interprovincial or international transportation interests,[22] demonstrated that anglophone capital was prepared to mobilize against the extension of Caisse ownership and influence. In the case of giant multinationals with operations in Quebec's manufacturing sector, corporations such as General Motors, Ford Motor Company, and IBM, the size of the investment required to exercise influence as a *shareholder* precludes this possibility.

To summarize this section, the fact that a preponderance of the Caisse's private sector investments are placed in corporations with significant non-Quebec operations (and in some cases with no Quebec operations whatever) does not signify that the Caisse has failed to apply savings generated in the province to Quebec-centred economic development. The opportunities for direct investment in Quebec-based corporations are limited both in number and by the fact that the Caisse's role as fiduciary eliminates the possibility of the agency operating as a source of risk capital for businesses with uncertain prospects. As demonstrated in Table 4.7, the Caisse does have important holdings in dozens of Quebec-based corporations. Thus, the question for supporters of the Caisse's equity activities is whether the agency contributes *enough* toward channelling savings generated in the province toward indigenous economic development. In answering this question, quantitative measures of the Caisse's investment distribution provide only a partial picture. Specific cases illustrate the catalytic role the agency has played in Quebec's economic development.

(2) The Caisse as Catalyst

From the Caisse's creation in the mid-1960s it has been expected that the capital invested by the agency may in some circumstances be used to support industrial transformation of the Quebec economy.[23] In other words, the Caisse should be prepared to act as a catalyst, an agent instrumental in effecting change while itself remaining unaltered, providing part of the capital required for an undertaking directed by some other party or parties. Thus, the entrepreneurial function, involving effective control over the organization and execution of an economic project, would be vested elsewhere. Precisely from where direction for such Caisse-supported projects would come has never been settled.

While guarantees of independence contained in the Caisse's charter formally insulate the agency from political pressures, the Caisse's management has demonstrated on several occasions a sympathy with the catalytic role envisaged for the agency by successive governments. A foremost instance of this was the pivotal role played by the Caisse in the reorganization of Quebec's food distribution sector. Through financial support and pressure at the managerial level the Caisse facilitated the merger of three medium-sized food retailers into the Provigo chain during the late 1960s. The agency's involvement in Provigo's expansion continued into the 1970s. The Caisse acquired 24 per cent of the shares of M. Loeb Ltd., a competing food retailer, and representation on the board of directors of that corporation, providing leverage that facilitated Provigo's takeover of Loeb in the mid-1970s, despite opposition from the existing controlling interest. As the major shareholder in Provigo, the Caisse rejected a 1977 takeover offer from Sobeys Stores, a retailing chain controlled by the Sobey family of Nova Scotia. Thus, the financial support of the Caisse has been instrumental, first in consolidating a francophone presence in Quebec's food distribution sector, and then in ensuring that control remained within the province.

More generally, during its first several years of operation the Caisse supported corporate mergers, assisting in the transition of closely-held businesses into public companies with shares traded on the stock exchange. This supportive role continues to be performed on occasion. Caisse support was crucial in enabling the Quebec furniture manufacturer, Artopex International, to go public in November 1985. Since the 1973 transformation of the SGF into a wholly state-owned enterprise, the industrial reorganization function largely has been assigned to this state holding company. Caisse participation in the recently created Power Financial Corporation, and cooperation with a group of Quebec-based financial institutions in the takeover of Trust Général du Canada, indicate that the Caisse's main reorganization objectives recently have concerned Quebec's financial sector.[24]

In the case of venture capital, involving investment in enterprises with a high growth potential but also carrying higher risks than investment in long-established firms, the Caisse's charter permits up to 7 per cent of the agency's assets to be invested in the shares of corporations that have not yielded at least a 4 per cent annual return on common shares in each of the five years preceding their purchase. This so-called "basket clause" enables the Caisse to support the launching of new enterprises in the province. To this point the Caisse's systematic participation in the area of venture capital has been limited to its 25 per cent ownership stake in Investissements Novacap, a venture capital firm of modest size. What is most interesting about Novacap, however, is that it constitutes a partnership between the Caisse and the SGF, each of which holds a 25 per cent ownership share (the remaining 50 per cent is divided between two private sector financial institutions, la Laurentienne and the National Bank of Canada). This relationship between functionally different organs of the Quebec state, the Caisse being a financier and the SGF an entrepreneur, along with francophone capital in the private sector, is significant primarily as an indication of the possibilities that exist for formal cooperation in financing economic development.

Compared to the mere possibilities prefigured in a formal relationship like Novacap, *informal* cooperation between the Caisse and other investors already has had important consequences for the Quebec economy, as shown in the case of Provigo's incorporation and subsequent expansion. The foremost illustration of an informal relationship between the Caisse and other principals to effect some specific change in the Quebec economy is, of course, the takeover of Domtar. In acquiring control over that publicly-traded company there was orchestration between the highest levels of Caisse and SGF management,[25] active cooperation on the part of Montreal businessman Paul Desmarais, whose Power Corporation holdings sold large blocks of shares to the Caisse, and the prior knowledge and support of the Parti Québécois government. The pivotal role played by the Caisse, the only state organ that could have financed a takeover through purchases on the stock market, demonstrated that the agency was prepared to cooperate in an acquisition project which was spawned out of the government's publicly-expressed dissatisfaction with Domtar's corporate behaviour (particularly the relocation of Domtar's Sifto division headquarters from Montreal to Toronto, and major capital expenditures in the mid-American region at a time when the PQ government was intent on increasing salt mining within the province) and the search by SGF, on instructions from the minister of industry, for a large corporate holding in order to stabilize its revenue position.

In playing a crucial supportive role in such projects as the consolidation of Provigo and the takeover of Domtar, the Caisse has satisfied the expectation that it will act as a catalyst for economic change in circumstances that do not compromise its fiduciary responsibility. Quantitative measures of Caisse investment in Quebec-based corporations fail to disclose this qualitative contribution that the agency has made in restructuring either the ownership profile or scale of economic activity in particular sectors. The sensitivity of Caisse management to economic objectives that go beyond the mere growth of its invested assets was demonstrated when Caisse chairman Jean Campeau went on record stating that the Caisse would consider investing in a Honda automobile plant if that automaker decided to locate in Quebec instead of Ontario.[26] While Honda ultimately chose an Ontario location for its $100 million investment, Campeau's intervention confirmed that Caisse management understands the agency's potential as a lever of economic development, and is willing to act on this awareness.

(3) The Caisse's Authority as an Investor

During debate on the legislation establishing the Caisse, Premier Lesage spoke of the "moral authority" he expected the Caisse's market interventions to carry. This went to the heart of the Caisse's role. The whole point behind an investment agency, inspired by western European precedents, as opposed to the "pay as you go" fund first proposed by Ottawa in the 1963-1964 pension plan negotiations, was to create a lever whereby the state could influence the province's capital markets. The immediate goal, of course, was to reduce the dependence of the Quebec state on the financial syndicate which, for years, had controlled the placement of Quebec government bonds. But the remarks of Lesage and such cabinet ministers as Eric Kierans and Réne Lévesque and others during debate on the legislation establishing the Caisse reflected the expectation that the agency's participation in the province's capital markets would carry consequences beyond the simple substitution of public capital for private capital in financing the state. As a public sector agent and, in Lesage's words, "a more powerful (economic) lever than any we have had in the province up to now,"[27] the Caisse's market interventions would express the provincial interest in particular circumstances. Lesage suggested the scenario of a threatened takeover by foreign interests of an important Quebec-based corporation, in which case the investment resources of the Caisse could prove instrumental in preventing the alienation of control. More generally, the Caisse would express the provincial interest in its investment behaviour through both the stabilization role it was expected to play regarding the market for provincial securities and by the sheer size which its assets were expected to reach.

The effectiveness of the Caisse shareholdings as an instrument of public policy would require that its authority as an investor with a special relationship to the public interest be recognized as legitimate by the business community. Compelled to operate within investment markets dominated by the private sector (the stock exchanges, the corporate and government bond markets), the Caisse has had to achieve and maintain the acceptance of the financial and business sectors. Failure to maintain this legitimacy, a subjective condition, has palpable consequences. This was demonstrated after the Domtar takeover when the Caisse, because of an alleged violation of Ontario's securities regulations, was suspended from trading on the Toronto Stock Exchange, and in the conflict between the Caisse and management of Canadian Pacific, Canada's second largest industrial corporation, over board representation (i.e., anglophone capital and the federal government mobilized in support of restrictions on the Caisse's investment capacity).

These particular cases of conflict between the Caisse and private sector actors raised to prominence the more general issue of the perceived legitimacy of Caisse participation in the private sector of the economy. Survey data recently has become available, demonstrating the gulf that separates the perceptions of the anglophone business community (represented in the objections raised by such major firms as CP, Alcan, and Dominion Textile to Caisse representation on their respective boards of directors) from those of both private sector clients of the Caisse and the francophone business community. Wide differences exist in the perception of the appropriate goals of the Caisse and its corporate behaviour. These differences disappear, however, when respondents are asked about the agency's relationship to the provincial government.

Whereas the anglophone business class overwhelmingly objects to the Caisse's economic development role, and does not consider that the Caisse has made a significant contribution to the development of Quebec businesses, the perceptions of francophone businessmen and clients of the Caisse are quite different. These latter groups support the economic development mandate of the Caisse, though not by wide margins, and agree that the investment activities of the Caisse have strengthened

TABLE 4.9
Business Community Perceptions Regarding the Investment Role of the Caisse de dépôt et placement du Québec (per cent)

The Economic Development Goal of the Caisse

Q.1 The Caisse de dépôt should not have as part of its legislative mandate the promotion of economic development.

	Clients	Francophones	Anglophones	Total
Agree	41	44	64	56
Disagree	59	52	31	40
N*	27	48	67	115

Q.2 Through its investments, the Caisse has contributed significantly to the development of Quebec business.

	Clients	Francophones	Anglophones	Total
Agree	78	48	19	31
Disagree	0	38	45	42

The Corporate Behavior of the Caisse

Q.3 All things considered, the Caisse de dépôt is one of the most respected investment institutions in Canada.

	Clients	Francophones	Anglophones	Total
Agree	67	58	30	42
Disagree	15	27	34	31

Q.4 The Caisse should be able to enter takeover agreements with private interests (like Brascan).

	Clients	Franco-phones	Anglo phones	Sympathizers**	Total
Against	59	57	90	63	76

Q.5 The Caisse should be able to enter takeover agreements with other state agencies (as in the case of Domtar).

	Clients	Franco-phones	Anglo phones	Sympathizers**	Total
Against	89	85	91	78	89

TABLE 4.9
(Continued)

Q.6 The Caisse should be able to place its representatives on . . .

	Clients	Franco-phones	Anglo phones	Sympathizers**	Total
. . . Boards of Directors.					
Agree	52	60	52	65	56
. . . Executive Committees.					
Agree	15	23	15	28	18

The Caisse/Government Relationship

Q.7 The Caisse is not sufficiently independent of the Quebec government.

	Clients	Franco-phones	Anglo phones	Sympathizers**	Total
Agree	78	81	82	76	82
Disagree	11	13	2	9	6

Q.8 A dominant shareholding by the Caisse de dépôt constitutes, or may constitute, a step toward gradual nationalization.

	Clients	Franco-phones	Anglo phones	Sympathizers**	Total
Agree	78	77	85	78	82
Disagree	19	21	12	22	15

* The sampling population is 115 for all of the tables. Column percentages may not total 100 because non-responses have been omitted. All the tables are adapted from Marcel Côte et Léon Courville, "La perceptions de la Caisse de dépôt et placement du Québec par les chefs d'entreprises", Tables 2, 3, 7, 9; in Claude E. Forget (ed.), *La Caisse de dépôt et placement du Québec* (Montreal: C.D. Howe Institute, 1984), pp. 74-84.

** The sympathizer category comprises those CEOs who support the Caisse's economic development mandate.

Quebec businesses. Similarly, while only 30 per cent of the anglophone respondents concur with the statement that the Caisse is one of the most respected investment institutions in Canada, 67 per cent of the Caisse's clients and 58 per cent of francophone respondents agree that the Caisse has this high respectability. Evidently, the perceived legitimacy of the Caisse's private sector investment activities is not shared by all segments of the business community. The difference of views between anglophone and francophone CEOs provides some confirmation of the proposition that the equity investment activities of the Caisse do not represent a challenge to private capital accumulation and corporate autonomy *per se*, but may in some cases challenge non-francophone control in the private sector of the Quebec economy.

Interestingly, there is an apparent convergence of views between the francophone and anglophone business communities about the related questions of Caisse representation on the board of directors of a private sector corporation, and the relationship of the Caisse to the provincial government. While a majority of respondents in each business category (francophone, anglophone, and clients of the Caisse) agree that the Caisse should be entitled to the normal prerogative of a major shareholder, namely, representation on the board of directors, only a third as many CEOs, whether francophone, anglophone or clients of the Caisse, consider that the Caisse should have representation at the executive committee level. Moreover, there is both a consensus that the Caisse is not sufficiently independent of the Quebec government, and a high level of agreement among francophones, anglophones and clients of the Caisse that a large ownership share held by that agency may represent a step toward gradual nationalization. Thus, even among francophone CEOs, who are generally sympathetic to the economic development role of the Caisse, there is strong opposition to cooperation between the Caisse and other organizations, whether public or private, where the objective is corporate control.

As interesting as the points of consensus and disagreement in the attitudes of anglophone and francophone CEOs is the fact that a considerable segment of the business community, the sympathizer category, expresses support for the economic development role of the Caisse (40 per cent; or 46 of 115 respondents) while objecting to some of the instrumentalities through which this mandate has been pursued. The distribution of responses received for Q.4 through Q.6 indicates that sympathizers are not remarkably more likely than CEOs as a whole to support Caisse participation in the control of private sector corporations. Moreover, sympathizers are only marginally less likely than anglophone CEOs (the least sympathetic category of respondents) to agree that the Caisse is not sufficiently independent of the Quebec government. Thus, the business community is able to divide on the question of whether the agency ought to operate as a tool of economic nationalism without a coextensive division on the issue of Caisse participation in corporate decision-making. The fact that sympathizers are not significantly less likely than CEOs as a whole to have reservations regarding both Caisse control over private sector corporations and the agency's relationship to the provincial government is plausibly explained. The Caisse's sympathizers view it as a pool of capital that stands in a supportive relationship to the private sector of the provincial economy. But as Pierre Lortie, former president of the Montreal Stock Exchange, has observed, this appreciation of the Caisse as *financier* does not signify approval of the agency as *dirigeant*.[28]

In summary, the survey data reported above reflect a division between francophone and anglophone capital that was evident in the 1982 debate on *The Corporate Shareholding Limitation Act*. Twice as many francophone CEOs as anglophone CEOs in the Quebec economy agree that the Caisse is one of the most respected investment institutions in Canada (58 per cent v. 30 per cent), a difference that suggests the greater legitimacy accorded the Caisse's direct investment role by the francophone business community. At the same time a consensus exists across language groups that the Caisse should not go beyond the role of passive investor, and that its investment behaviour should be determined independently of the economic preferences of the current government. What emerges from the pattern of private sector attitudes is that the Caisse has achieved only a limited success in establishing for itself a position of authority on the province's capital markets. Even among francophone CEOs a significant minority (44 per cent) challenges the proposition that the Caisse shareholdings should operate as an instrument of economic policy. Even when client firms of the Caisse are excluded from the population of francophone CEOs, the difference between the language groups is negligible (60 per cent of francophones v. 64 per cent of anglophones).

(4) Performance

Private sector investment funds seek a competitive rate of return on their invested capital, while at the same time attempting to reduce the exposure of their asset portfolio to downturns in the economic situation of particular investments or sectors of the economy. This latter objective is accomplished through the disbursement of investments, thereby reducing the risk of suffering a serious overall loss in the event of the poor performance of any single or small set of investments. The evidence indicates that the Caisse's financial performance generally has been superior to that of the Canada Pension Plan (the assets of the CPP are invested exclusively in government securities) and most other public pension investment agencies in Canada.[29] But it does appear that the equity portfolio of the Caisse is considerably more concentrated than is typical of pension funds.

The Caisse's return on invested capital of 10.1 per cent in 1984 was considerably less than the unweighted average of 16 per cent achieved both by Canada's five major banks and by the country's four largest trust companies. Given the different investment profiles of banks and trust companies on the one hand and pension funds on the other, a more meaningful comparison is between the Caisse and other pension funds. Table 4.10 compares the recent financial performance of the Caisse to that of the CPP and the Ontario Municipal Employees Retirement System (OMERS), the latter being the country's largest trusted pension fund (assets of CAN$4.3 billion, 1984). The superior financial performance of the Caisse provides no support for the view that political considerations have resulted in inefficient investment behaviour.

On portfolio diversification, the evidence is somewhat more ambiguous. In 1985, the Caisse held shares in 119 different companies. The 10 largest of these holdings together accounted for 42 per cent of the total market value of shares held by the Caisse, compared with 24 per cent for the 10 largest equity investments of OMERS. Whether the less diversified equity portfolio of the Caisse signifies a willingness to incur greater risk in order to promote provincial economic development objectives is not clear from this evidence alone. The corporations that constitute this group of 10 largest equity holdings include two of Canada's largest banks and eight industrial corporations, all of which place among the country's 50 largest industrial companies.[30] None of these investments can be considered a "Quebec-corporation," following the definition provided earlier.

Summary: The Social Return on State Capital

Analysis of the corporate performance of Telesat, the CDC and of the private sector investments of the Caisse reveals a mixed record of successes and failures in pursuing public policy goals. With the integration of Telesat into Telecom Canada, the terrestrially-based carriers are assured of control over commercial competition from this competing technology. The federal government's policy expectations for Telesat are evidently limited to the backward industrial linkages generated through the corporation's satellite acquisitions, and management has been able to treat this Canadian content expectation as a recompensable cost.

TABLE 4.10
The Rate of Return on Invested Capital for the Caisse, the CPP and OMERS, 1978-1985

		1985	1978-85
a)	Overall Rate of Return		
	Caisse	24%	13.9
	CPP	10	8.4
	OMERS	24	12.3
b)	Canadian Equities Portfolio of the Caisse*	27.1	18.1
c)	TSE 300 Index	25.1	18.3

Sources: Caisse de dépôt et placement, *Financial Statements and Financial Statistics*, 1985; Health and Welfare Canada, *Canada Pension Plan, Statistical Bulletin*, 1984-85; Ontario Municipal Employees Retirement Board, *Inventory of Investments*, December 31, 1985.

* Between 1968 and 1985, the period during which the Caisse has invested in equities, the average annual rate of return on this portfolio has been 12.6 per cent, compared with 11.1 per cent for the TSE 300 Index.

In the case of the CDC, the federal government's ill-defined policy objectives for the corporation were blocked by management's early assertion of decision-making autonomy (an autonomy supported by the Department of Finance) and by the government's complete failure to systematically provide policy signals to the corporation (for example, through annual cabinet review of the CDC's corporate strategy and performance). On balance, the CDC experiment in mixed ownership has resulted in dollar costs to the taxpaying public (through a real loss on the federal government's original investment of $250 million and the income foregone with the transfer of Polymer to the CDC) and antagonism between the federal government and the business community over the corporation's role in Ottawa's episodic lurches in the direction of an industrial strategy. The CDC has provided very marginal social benefits in the form of *some* patriation of corporate ownership (though the most prominent case of this was an incidental consequence of the NEP, and not of unequivocal public policy signals embedded in the corporation's charter or emanating from the state shareholder) and the development of a large pool of Canadian equity capital.

The Caisse's record of performance through its shareholdings has been quite different. Through its equity investments in dozens of Quebec-based corporations the Caisse has channelled savings generated in the province toward indigenous economic development. Moreover, the Caisse has acted as a catalyst in specific instances of industrial reorganization in the Quebec economy. The agency's pivotal role in the consolidation of Provigo, and in financing the Domtar takeover, are the two most outstanding examples of this catalytic function. Even so, the Caisse has not compromised its fiduciary responsibility to the millions of Quebec citizens whose compulsory contributions it invests. As a proportion of total investments its equity portfolio is heavily weighted toward blue chip stocks, representing shares in corporations with considerable operations outside of Quebec. Moreover, the Caisse's financial performance generally has been superior to that of the Canada Pension Plan and most other public pension investment agencies in Canada.[31]

The Caisse has been less successful, however, in establishing its legitimacy as an investor in the private sector of the economy. While the representatives of francophone capital tend to be more sympathetic to the economic development role of the Caisse shareholdings than their anglophone counterparts, there is still considerable opposition within Quebec's francophone private sector to the idea that the Caisse shareholdings should be used as an instrument of economic policy. Furthermore, the francophone business community was not significantly less wary of the links between the PQ government and the Caisse's investment policy than were the representatives of anglophone capital. Thus, while the Caisse's investment record may demonstrate that it stands in a supportive relationship to Quebec's francophone bourgeoisie, the members of this class show no more disposition than their anglophone counterparts to allow the Caisse a share in the decision-making of its shareholdings.

Chapter 5

Lessons from the Past

The original expectations of unobtrusive influence that Liberal governments had in creating Telesat and the CDC, and which the Lesage and subsequent Quebec governments have held regarding the Caisse's private sector investments in the provincial economy, have run up against organizational features of the MOC that limit the ability of government to influence corporate behaviour. No evidence was found to support the proposition that managers of an MOC occasionally experience ambivalence in their roles in consequence of the divergent expectations of the state shareholder and private capital. At least in the decision situations examined, trade-offs between business and political values did not occur as a psychological balancing act. Instead, the state's public policy expectations typically were treated by management as intrusions upon corporate autonomy, to be resisted as far as possible or accommodated with compensation. In other words, where management was responsive to the state's non-commercial goals for the corporation this was not due to the partial assimilation of a state agent role. Rather, it was due to either coercion or management's perception that the costs of complete resistance exceeded those of accommodation.

The limits on the state shareholder's capacity to pursue public policy goals through the mixed ownership corporation are understood more concretely from examination of several decision situations where the preferences of the state and private capital were in conflict. In each case a perceived attempt by the state to influence corporate behaviour in a way considered by management to prejudice the commercial competitiveness or corporate autonomy of the firm was opposed as an illegitimate intrusion into corporate decision-making. In those cases where the state shareholder was successful in influencing corporate behaviour along lines opposed by management and/or private shareholders, success came at a price. Indeed, the price of forced compliance (coercion) with the state's preferences appears to be crisis in the relationship between the state and private capital in the mixed enterprise, while the price of induced compliance (suasion) is compensation.

These decisions involving conflict demonstrated that typically a three-cornered relationship exists between the state shareholder, private capital and management of the MOC. In other words, it is somewhat misleading to view the decisions of a mixed ownership firm in light of the tension between the public policy goals of a government and the profitability goals of private capital. The interests of private capital (which, as the case of Telesat showed, may *not* involve profitability and market competitiveness of the MOC) are refracted through management's goal of maintaining corporate autonomy. This was evident from interviews with managers of both Telesat and the CDC. There was, however, an important difference between the two sets of actors in that CDC managers alluded regularly to their fiduciary responsibility to the corporation's shareholders *as a whole* (signifying the profitability concern of private investors), while Telesat actors defended corporate autonomy from government intervention by reference to the business values expressed in the corporation's charter. In other words, management's resistance to government influence may be based on different reference points, but in each of the conflict cases examined business values were invoked in defence of corporate autonomy.

Although the findings of three case studies do not provide conclusive evidence for valid generalizations about this triadic relationship, it does appear that management's fiduciary responsibility to take all reasonable care to protect the invested capital of the firm's shareholders operates as the most effective check on government control. This check is largely absent in the case of Telesat, whose corporate charter assigns the federal government a privileged role in the capital expenditure decisions of the firm, the selection of the corporation's CEO, and the transfer of ownership shares. Moreover, Telesat's ownership structure is unlike that of either the CDC or the equity holdings of the Caisse in that it involves a small number of shareholders and the firm's equity is not traded publicly. This means that, practically, Telesat represents a partnership of state capital and several commercially oriented telecommunications firms (but particularly Telecom Canada), and thus management's fiduciary responsibility to its shareholders is significantly different than it would be if Telesat were a public company. The ownership rights of thousands of private shareholders in a MOC confronts a government that has non-commercial goals for the firm with the *general* interest of private capital. At least in the case of the CDC (and the debate over Bill S-31 and the Caisse would seem to confirm this), this general interest proved an effective shield against state intervention. Incorporation under general business legislation or, if created by a special act, ambiguity in regard to the relationship of the MOC to public policy reinforce the primacy of business values in the firm's operations.

The form of the state's relationship to the MOC determines the available channels for attempts by the state shareholder to influence corporate behaviour. The channels of government influence range from the most general and indirect, applying to all businesses which, because of their size, location or activities, must anticipate state reaction to some types of behaviour, to those that are institutionalized and direct, as in the case of a Crown corporation. Like Crown corporations, MOCs incorporated under special legislation also have an institutionalized and direct relationship to the state by the terms of the charter under which they operate, while in the case of MOCs incorporated under general business law, the channels of state influence are basically the same as those through which any shareholder must operate (for example, attempting to influence the membership of the corporation's board of directors).

It must be emphasized, however, that because the state shareholder has a status different from other shareholders under the terms of the legislation creating the MOC, this does not necessarily signify greater government influence than in the case of a publicly-traded company in which the state has acquired an ownership share. Nor is the size of the state's shareholding a reliable guide to government's ability to use the MOC as a policy instrument. Ottawa's 48 per cent ownership share in the CDC did not translate into compliance by management and the board of directors with the government's expressed preferences for the chairmanship and board membership. Nor was the Caisse's 20 per cent equity stake in Domtar before the 1981 takeover considered by the PQ government to be sufficient to sensitize Domtar's management to the provincial government's views on new corporate investment and the transfer of operations out of

Quebec. Government influence on the MOC is highly *situational*, depending on several factors relating to both the firm's internal organization and the political economic environment in which it operates.

One can only speculate as to how a company's receptivity to state influence might vary with different management actors. In other words, given some degree of ambiguity in the corporation's mandate, how far are decisions on whether to attend to political or business signals determined by the personal orientations of managers, and how far by structural features of the corporation and its relationship to markets (i.e., the market for its product and the market for financing)? The main thrust of this study has been the examination of these structural limits on state control of the mixed ownership firm. Based on the analyses of Telesat and the CDC, it was observed that the federal government's initial selection of senior managers reinforced the business values expressed in the charter of each corporation. It can at least be argued that the public policy goals set out in the charter of these firms, and which can be discerned from the respective origins of Telesat and the CDC, might have been given greater emphasis by different managers. Certainly the resistance that greeted the federal government's abortive effort to instal Maurice Strong as chairman of the CDC demonstrated that all parties considered that the individuals involved in the corporation's decision-making made a difference in terms of corporate behaviour. Similarly, the conflict between CP management and the Caisse was based on private sector concern that even a corporation with no statutory relationship to public policy could find itself subject to political pressures expressed internally (i.e., through the board of directors).

Even if one grants that the particular actors involved in managing the MOC have not been irrelevant to corporate behaviour, this does not suggest that management attitude and corporate structure are equally important in determining how receptive the MOC will be to policy signals coming from the government shareholder. Management receptivity to non-commercial objectives for the firm will inevitably be tempered by the interests (and legal rights) of private shareholders. But what if, as in the case of Telesat, the private shareholders appear not to have any particular interest in the profitability of the MOC? In such a case the attitude of management—how they resolve the ambiguity that may be created by the MOC's charter and/or simply by the fact of operating a self-financing company in a competitive market while the state shareholder holds certain expectations for the firm that impair its commercial performance – assumes increased significance.

The sources of resistance to state control that are inherent in the MOC point to a contradiction between state entrepreneurship and capitalist business norms. This contradiction becomes particularly clear when conflict spills over from the mixed ownership corporation to engage a larger configuration of interests on the issue of the proper spheres of the state and private capital in the economy. The cases of decisions examined in this study were characterized by a tendency toward the spillover of conflict, with the resolution of divergent preferences for the firm influenced by the scope of conflict. Failure to contain conflict within the MOC has meant broader private sector opposition to state control of the firm, and in some cases has involved division within the state (as the Telesat/TCTS Membership Agreement placed the CRTC in conflict with the federal cabinet, and the issue of the CDC's relationship to public policy was a source of division within the federal government throughout the 1970s). Thus, the state's ability to pursue public policy goals through the mixed ownership corporation appears to be limited by this observed tendency for conflict to spread beyond the bounds of the firm, mobilizing a wider set of interested parties around an issue with higher stakes for business/state relations than those attendant upon the immediate cause of dispute.

An additional factor that appears to influence the receptivity of private sector actors to state participation in, or influence on, the decision-making of an MOC is the prevailing culture of business-government relations. This study has alluded to the constraints of "business ideology", as in the analysis of the attitudes of the Canadian business community toward the investment activities of the Caisse. Although the concept has not been examined in a systematic way, it appears to be significant in explaining cross-national differences in reactions from the private sector to the state's investment activities. For example, Eckel and Vining examine the correlation between business community *perception*[1] of increased state intervention in the affairs of a MOC and the market value of the corporation's stock, and find that an increase in the former is associated with a decrease in the latter. But this relationship is neither universal nor directly causal. In Singapore, for example, state investment in a corporation generally does not result in a decrease in the market value of the mixed enterprise's stock. This can be attributed to the expectation, based on past practice, that the state will privatize its investment when its equity support is no longer required. As the largest single source of investment in the

Singapore economy, the state is expected to assume an entrepreneurial role in support of economic development, while not threatening the primacy of *private* capital accumulation.[2] A similar receptivity is observed in Japan, where business community reaction to direct investment by the state is not determined by an expectation that government intervention means inevitable bureaucratization and inefficiency, and a consequent deterioration in the business orientation of a corporation. More generally, what Chalmers Johnson describes as the Japanese control ideology, namely, an interventionist view shared by state personnel and business leaders, reinforced by cross-penetration of elites and such corporatist institutions as government advisory councils, contributes to the acceptance of forms of intervention and public-private cooperation that are considered anomalous in many western political economies.[3] Overall, it is fair to say that the impact of political culture on the legitimate boundaries and forms of economic intervention by the state remains unexamined.[4]

In view of the apparent limits on the state's ability to influence decision-making in the MOC, one is entitled to ask what are the social returns on the public's invested capital. These vary across the three organizations examined in this study, from the relative success of Telesat in promoting the growth of a domestic manufacturing capacity in satellites, through the supportive relationship of the Caisse shareholdings to Quebec's francophone business community, to the nebulous social returns the Canadian public received on its investment in the CDC. Based on the three cases studied, the factors determining the effectiveness of the MOC as a policy instrument can be summarized as follows:

1. the scale of the firm's operations (state influence on the behaviour of a small firm is likely to mobilize less private sector opposition than in the case of a nationally important corporation);

2. the pattern of private sector shareholding (a public company, with shares held by the general investing public, is more resistant to state control than a joint-stock company with ownership divided between the state and a small set of private shareholders);

3. the existence of a clearly defined mandate (incorporation under special legislation does not necessarily render an organization more amenable to state influence, but

specification of the state's relationship to the decision process facilitates accommodation of the state's public policy goals for the MOC);

4. the degree of agreement within the state on the relationship of the MOC to public policy (division within the government, or between parts of the state representing divergent policy views, reduces the likelihood of state influence on corporate behaviour); and

5. the degree to which the states' non-commercial preferences for the MOC are supported by important segments of the business community, as illustrated by the support of Pierre Lortie and others in Quebec's francophone corporate elite for a *large* equity role (though not control) for the Caisse.

In the case of Telesat, the state's relative success in pursuing policy goals through the satellite corporation can be ascribed to the small scale of the firm's operations, the fact of a limited number of other shareholders whose interests are in controlling telecommunications competition rather than earning a profit on their investment in Telesat, and a corporate charter that provides the state shareholder with potential levers of influence in corporate decision-making. The social returns on the Caisse's equity investments have been based on a different combination of factors. These are, principally, the consensus within Quebec's state elite on the province-building project in which the Caisse is a key engine of economic development and the support of a significant segment of Quebec's francophone bourgeoisie (including prominent individuals like Paul Desmarais, Yves Pratte, Roland Peladeau, and Pierre Lortie) for the *general* framework of nationalist goals in which the Caisse's investment role is situated.[5] Finally, the complete imperviousness of the CDC to the influence attempts of the federal government resulted from a negative loading on each of the factors listed. Robert Couzin's 1971 prediction that "in the absence of policy, the CDC will remain a not-so-gratuitous curiosity,"[6] turned out to be remarkably accurate.

Points 1, 3, 4 and 5 also apply, though not necessarily to the same degree, to Crown corporations. This raises the question that is begged at various points in this study, namely, what is special about the MOC as a policy instrument? What does it do well, and what poorly, and are its possibilities and problems significantly different from those of Crown corporations? How can Ottawa's "success" in using PetroCanada as part of its nationalist strategy for the energy sector at the same time as it was experiencing "failure" in transforming the CDC into a more controllable instrument of industrial policy be explained? This study has not attempted a systematic comparison of MOCs and Crown corporations, so the following observations should be taken in the spirit of speculation in which they are offered.

First, it needs to be emphasized that, in most circumstances, there are other policy instruments that could readily substitute for the MOC. A typical scenario has government wanting to encourage development in some particular sector of the economy or to restructure the economy in some way. The traditional instruments of tax incentives to businesses, regulation, direct subsidies and loans, and even state ownership all are possible means for pursuing these goals. And, indeed, the simultaneous use of some combination of policy instruments is probable. The decision to create the MOC appears to be based on an original expectation that it will provide a relatively direct lever for government influence, while stopping short of state ownership and the displacement of private capital. This influence may not be through active participation in the corporation's decision-making, but perhaps may involve the simple fact of determining where state capital is invested (e.g., a particular sector of the economy, as in the case of Telesat, or in a particular province, as with some of the Caisse shareholdings).

A government's ability to influence the behaviour of the MOC after the initial investment is, however, highly situational. The degree of state ownership does not provide a reliable guide to this influence. This was dramatically illustrated by the inability of the federal government to overcome the resistance of CDC management and the board of directors at a time when Ottawa held about 48 per cent of that corporation's equity. In addition to the internal barriers to government influence in that particular case (the long pattern of non-intervention, the legal rights of private shareholders), there was virtually no significant business support for a transformed CDC which, to paraphrase Pierre Trudeau, would operate in the industrial economy as PetroCanada did in the petroleum sector. Moreover, the business community was not indifferent to the fate of the CDC, generally rejecting the idea of state control. Nor was the business community indifferent toward Caisse participation in either Domtar or CP. Indifference may increase the ability of a government to impose its policy goals on the MOC by reducing the political costs associated with the opposition of business interests not directly involved with the MOC. But *outside* interest sometimes may be a resource, as was true of the support that the Caisse received from prominent members of Quebec's francophone business community when Ottawa proposed, through Bill S-31, to limit the ability of the provinces to invest in some publicly-traded companies.

In view of the problems that governments have encountered in trying to use the MOC for purposes not concurred in by managers and/or private investors, it is worth asking what, if anything, the MOC does particularly well. First, at least where the MOC has been created as a result of the state's purchase of equity in an existing corporation, as was true of the Alberta government's acquisition of Pacific Western Airlines and of the Caisse's shareholdings, the MOC appears to be characterized by greater *reversibility* (i.e., withdrawal of state involvement) than is true of a Crown corporation or MOC operating under a special statute. Second, there may be circumstances where equity capital is needed in a particular industrial sector or in the economy generally, and where the state is a necessary source for this financial support. The former chairman of the Montreal Stock Exchange, Pierre Lortie, made this argument when he observed that the capital structure of Canadian business relies too heavily on comparatively more expensive loan financing, and that, "in its auxiliary role in the financial markets, the government should be more active in the area of capital stock."[7] Finally,it may be that the MOC, which unlike a Crown corporation is not legally an agent of the state, allows for a more effective isolation of the costs that accompany the social goals a government may wish to pursue through the corporation. This, however, could be done in some other way, as through the performance contracts that have long existed between the French government and some private sector firms, a form of regulation that does not require the state to have an ownership share in the firm.

In conclusion, a 1975 prognostication that "(the) CDC may very well be an early prototype of a model to which all but the most doctrinaire capitalist or socialist economies may turn,"[8] must be viewed with some scepticism based on the cases examined in this study. Those who assume that a state ownership share means, *ipso facto*, that an MOC has at least the potentiality of a special relationship to public policy would do well to consider these lessons from the past.

Notes

Preface

1. See A. Boardman et al., "An Overview of Mixed Enterprises in Canada" (University of B.C., Faculty of Commerce and Business Administration, mimeo, 1983), in W. Stanbury and E.C. Elford, *Mixed Enterprises in Canada,* paper presented to the Seminar on Crown Corporations, Royal Commission on the Economic Union and Development Prospects for Canada, Ottawa, June 1, 1984.

2. Stanbury and Elford, *op. cit.* pp. 17-24.

3. See *ibid* , Table 2, p. 24.

4. *Ibid.*, p. 37.

Chapter 1

1. Marshall E. Dimock, "Les Enterprises Mixtes". *National Municipal Review* (November 1931), pp. 639-641.

2. For a much more detailed analysis of the origins of Telesat, the CDC and the Caisse, see Stephen Brooks, *Direct*

Investment by the State: The Mixed Ownership Corporation in Canada, Ph.D. thesis, Carleton University, Ottawa, 1985, Chapters 2, 3, and 4.

3. In the case of the legislation establishing COMSAT, the United States administration found itself negotiating with a single senator, Robert S. Kerr, chairman of the Senate Aeronautical and Space Sciences Committee, over the ownership and control structure of the proposed satellite corporation. See the account of events in Herman Schwartz, "Governmentally Appointed Directors in a Private Corporation - The Communications Satellite Act of 1962", *Harvard Law Review*, Vol. 79, No. 2, December 1965, especially pp. 351-52.

4. According to one principal who was involved with the CDC at its inception, the government's idea that the corporation should be based in Vancouver was a concession to western Liberals who had opposed the CDC concept. Personal interview, January 20, 1984.

5. *CDC Act*, s.2.

Chapter 2

1. For a representative illustration of the "ownership makes a difference" argument see Robert M. Spann, "Public versus Private Provision of Governmental Services", in Thomas E. Borcherding, ed., *Budgets and Bureaucrats: The Sources of Government Growth* (Durham, North Carolina: Duke University Press, 1977), pp. 71-89.

2. Quoted in *The Economist*, "Balladur denationalises the banks, if not the bankers", May 24, 1986, p. 85. For a representative illustration of the "ownership does not make a difference argument" see Harvey Feigenbaum, "Public Enterprise in Comparative Perspective", *Comparative Politics*, Vol. 15, No. 1, October 1982, pp. 101-122.

3. See Jean-Pierre C. Anastassopoulos, "The French Experience: Conflicts with Government", in R. Vernon and Y. Aharoni, (eds.), *State-Owned Enterprise in the Western Economies* (London: Croom Helm, 1981), pp. 99-117.

4. See Oystein Noreng, "State-Owned Oil Companies: Western Europe", in R. Vernon and Y. Aharoni (eds.), *State-Owned Enterprise in the Western Economics* (London: Croom Helm, 1981), pp. 135-136.

5. Personal interview, April 26, 1985.

6. A typical statement of government expectations was expressed by the minister of finance, Edgar Benson, at the time Bill C-219 was introduced: "Able and experienced entrepreneurs will direct the corporation's operations to areas of critical importance in economic development – to high technology industry, to resource utilization, to northern-oriented companies and to industries where Canada has a special competitive advantage."

7. *CDC Act*, s.6(1).

8. Personal interview; December 9, 1983.

9. Personal interview; December 9, 1983.

10. Personal interview; December 19, 1983.

11. The OSC estimated that the Caisse's ownership share in Domtar went from 25.5 per cent before July 31, 1981, to 41.4 per cent by August 11. See Amy Booth, "Quebec's big affair with Domtar", *The Financial Post* (February 12, 1983), p. 6.

12. See M. Nadeau, "La Cour donne raison a la Caisse: Ouellet reclamait la divulgation des transactions", *Le Devoir*, 12 août 1982, p. 7. Since 1982, the Caisse has published a list of its private sector investments in its annual report. This, however, is done voluntarily, and not in recognition of a legal obligation.

13. Personal interview; January 20, 1984.

14. Canada Development Corporation, "Preliminary Prospectus dated March 16, 1983", p. 51.

15. Personal interview; December 12, 1983.

16. Henry Mintzberg, *Power in and around Organizations* (Englewood Cliffs: Prentice-Hall, 1983), p. 69.

17. At bottom, the interconnection issue is about the structure of competition in the long distance and business telecommunications market. For a discussion from an industrial organization perspective, see Christopher Green, *Canadian Industrial Organization and Policy* (Toronto: McGraw-Hill Ryerson, 1980), pp. 232-234.

18. Personal interview; December 12, 1983.

19. Personal interview; December 12, 1983.

20. Personal interview; December 9, 1983.

21. In ruling on the Telesat/TCTS membership agreement the CRTC observed: "As a member of TCTS, decisions about satellite system design, capital costs and performance requirements as well as proposed terms, conditions and rates for satellite services would be subject to the unanimous approval of TCTS members and hence the veto of any one of them". See CRTC, Telecom. Decision CRTC 77-10, *Telesat Canada, Proposed Agreement with Trans-Canada Telephone System*. reported in *The Canada Gazette*, Part 1, September 3, 1977, pp. 4838-4883.

22. Personal interview; December 9, 1983.

23. Personal interview; December 9, 1983.

24. *CDC Act*, s. 41. These *ex officio* members were not entitled to vote at meetings of the board of directors.

25. The irregular attendance of government members on CDC's board of directors, and the fact that lower ranking officials substituted for their deputy ministers (as is provided for by s.41(2) of the *CDC Act*) until 1981, was confirmed in several interviews. Personal interviews; December 19, 1983, January 20 and February 21, 1984.

26. Personal interview; December 19, 1983.

27. All the CDC management actors and directors interviewed were of the view that the formal link between the

government and the corporation, through the *ex officio* directors, did not operate as a channel for communication between the CDC and its largest shareholder.

28. Personal interview; December 19, 1983.

29. Personal interview; February 3, 1984.

30. In response to the statement, "The Caisse should be able to place its representatives on boards of directors," a majority of CEOs surveyed for a recent study agreed that this right should be accorded the Caisse (anglophone CEOs, 52 per cent; francophone CEOs, 60 per cent; client CEOs 52 per cent). See Marcel Cote et Leon Courville, "La perceptions de la Caisse de dépôt et placement du Québec par les chefs d'entreprises", Table 7: in Claude E. Forget (ed.), *La Caisse de dépôt et placement du Québec* (Montreal: C.D. Howe Institute, 1984), p. 81.

31. During the Senate Committee hearings on Bill S-31 the chairman of the Caisse, Jean Campeau, indicated that the Caisse had representation on the boards of "about 15 companies". He listed four of the corporations (Noranda, Brascade, Domtar, and Gaz Métropolitain), but in response to Senator Godfrey's request for a list of Caisse nominees who are not agency officials, Campeau would say only that they are prominent business people. While in its annual report for 1983 the Caisse discloses the publicly-traded corporations in which the agency holds equity, breaking with the past practice of secrecy, information on Caisse-nominated directors who are not Caisse officials remains unavailable.

32. This information is drawn from the Financial Post's *Directory of Directors* (1985).

33. The promotion of competitive economies of scale, through industry reorganization, has been an important goal of Quebec economic policy since the creation of the SGF in 1962. Aside from the Provigo case, the activities of the Caisse have not been central to this policy.

34. Personal interview; February 3, 1984.

35. Personal interview; February 3, 1984.

36. Personal interview; February 3, 1984.

37. Personal interview; February 2, 1984.

38. Catherine Eckel and Aidan Vining, "Toward a Positive Theory of Joint Enterprise", in W.T. Stanbury and Fred Thompson (eds.), *Managing Public Enterprises* (New York: Praeger, 1982), p. 215.

39. Personal interview; January 20, 1984.

40. Personal interviews; December 19, 1983, and January 20, 1984.

41. Personal interview; February 21, 1984.

42. Personal interview; January 20, 1984.

43. See the discussion in Chapter 4.

44. See Robert Steklasa, "CRTC rulings enrage Telesat", *Financial Post*, May 7, 1983.

Chapter 3

1. See Stephen Brooks, "The Mixed Ownership Corporation as an Instrument of Public Policy", *Comparative Politics* Vol. 19, No. 2 (January 1987), pp. 173-191.

2. Franco A. Grassini, "The Italian Enterprises: The Political Constraints", in Vernon and Aharoni (eds.), *State-Owned Enterprise in the Western Economies* (London: Croom Helm, 1981), pp. 70-84; Jean-Pierre Anastassopoulos, "The French Experience: Conflicts with Government", in *ibid.*, pp. 99-116; and R. Mazzolini, *Government Controlled Enterprises: International Strategic and Policy Decisions* (Toronto: John Wiley & Sons, 1979).

3. Canada, Senate Standing Committee on Legal and Constitutional Affairs, Proceedings, December 2, 1982, p. 35.

Hereafter cited as Senate, Standing Committee, *Proceedings*, date, page.

4. In the late 1970s the Quebec government approached Domtar with a proposal that the corporation cooperate with the government in developing the salt deposits on the Magdalen Islands. Domtar's management declined on commercial grounds and the government proceeded on its own through Soquem, a Crown corporation.

5. See the discussion in Chapter 4.

6. This unequivocal interpretation of "on a commercial basis" was repeated by every Telesat principal interviewed, with the exception of one of the government-appointed directors who expressed some mild misgivings about what he considered inadequate attention to social goals in the corporation's operating history. Personal interview, December 9, 1983.

7. Personal interviews, December 1,7,9, 1983.

8. Personal interviews, Decembe 1,7,9, 1983.

9. Personal interview, December 9, 1983.

10. Personal interview; April 26, 1985.

11. Personal interviews, December 7,9, 1983.

12. See Telesat Canada, *Annual Report*, 1979, p. 28.

13. Personal interview, December 12, 1983.

14. Personal interviews, December 1,9,12, 1983.

15. Doern and Brothers attribute to the government this window-on-the-industry reasoning, apparently based on no more than a remark the minister of communications, Jeanne Sauve, was reported to have made. In support of what is a rather major claim, they cite only the remarks attributed to Sauve in Frank Howard's column, "Bureaucrats", *Ottawa Citizen* (November 7, 1977), p. 2.

16. This contract required an amendment to the *Telesat Act* and, according to some Telesat actors, encountered some resistance within the cabinet on the grounds that the nationalistic goals of the domestic satellite corporation might thereby be compromised.

17. Personal interview, December 1, 1983.

18. See Telesat Canada, "Telesat Canada, Proposed Agreement with TransCanada Telephone System: Rationale – Motivation – Alternatives" (Ottawa: March 29, 1977, mimeo).

19. Difficulties in forecasting markets and, therefore, arriving at reliable estimates of future income has plagued satellite telecommunications since the beginning of commercial satellite broadcasting. This situation continues, as demonstrated in the recent collapse of the fledgling pay-TV market in Canada, one of the consequences of which has been a major loss of anticipated revenue for Telesat.

20. Personal interview, December 12, 1983.

21. The relevant passage of the memorandum of agreement (December 31, 1976) between Telesat and the TCTS reads: ". . . Telesat shall not build, own, operate, maintain or control any terrestrial transmission facilities in TCTS members' territories, except for the purpose of the operation and the control of the space segment of the system, and only then when such transmission facilities cannot be provided to Telesat's satisfaction by the TCTS members."

22. Personal interviews, December 1,12, 1983.

23. Personal interview, Decembe 9,12, 1983.

24. A long-time government appointee to Telesat's board argues that this is the government's primary expectation for Telesat, and that the Canadian content preference is a secondary goal advocated by DOC. Personal interview, December 9, 1983.

25. The competing industrial strategy and capital markets versions of the CDC are discussed in Chapter 3.

26. One senior bureaucrat who was interviewed for this study referred to long debates within the government during the 1970s over the appropriate role of the CDC. Personal interview, February 21, 1984.

27. This interventionism was most clearly manifested in the National Energy Program. Less concretely, the development of an industrial strategy was accorded priority in public statements by Herb Gray, the minister of industry, trade and commerce.

28. With the departure of such ministers as Turner, Macdonald, Gillespie and Sharp in the mid-1970s, the Priorities and Planning Committee of cabinet came increasingly to be dominated by the more interventionist wing of the Liberal Party.

29. Personal interview, February 21, 1984.

30. These facts were corroborated in a number of interviews with both management and state actors.

31. Personal interview, February 21, 1984.

32. Personal interview; April 22, 1985.

33. *Ibid.*

34. This interpretation is supported by the remarks of a senior economic official who was involved in the events of 1980-1981. Personal interview, February 21, 1984.

35. Personal interview, February 21, 1984.

36. Personal interview, February 21, 1984.

37. CDC management actors support the version of events chronicled by Peter Foster in his article, "The Battle of the Sectors", *Saturday Night* (March 1983), especially pages 27-30.

38. The investment community's reaction can be gauged from the decline in the market value of CDC shares which occurred during the period of the control crisis. In fact, CDC's stock declined in value by 8 per cent on a single day

(May 12), representing a decrease of $85 million in the corporation's market value.

39. This interpretation of the outcome is supported by both management actors, and the state official most intimately involved in the control crisis. Personal interviews, December 19 , 1983; January 20, 1984; February 21, 1984.

40. The currency of this negative view of the state as a commercial decision-maker is demonstrated in the continuing popularity of P. Mathias' book, *Forced Growth* (Toronto, 1971).

41. See my article entitled, "The State as Entrepreneur: From CDC to CDIC", *Canadian Public Administration* (Winter 1983), pp. 525-543.

42. Personal interviews; April 22, 1985.

43. *Ibid.*

44. In April 1974, the federal government invested $50 million in equity, completing the $250 million cash subscription authorized by the *CDC Act*.

45. Personal interview; April 22, 1985.

46. See Stephen Clarkson, *Canada and the Reagan Challenge* (Toronto: Lorimer, 1985), pp. 18-19.

47. Personal interview; April 22, 1985.

48. Société générale de financement, *Rapport Annuel*, 1982, p. 7.

49. Personal interview, February 2, 1984.

50. See Bernard Descoteaux, "Parizeau accuse la Domtar d'agir à l'encontre des intèrêts des Québécois", *Le Devoir*, 3 decembre, 1980, p. 1.

51. Personal interview, February 2, 1984.

52. See the summary of the OSC's investigation in Amy Booth, "Quebec's big affair with Domtar", *Financial Post* (February 12, 1983), p. 6.

53. Michel Nadeau, "Les actions de Domtar ont perdu 15% de leur valeur", *Le Devoir*, 20 août, 1981, p. 5.

54. Personal interview, February 2, 1984.

55. Quoted in Amy Booth, *op. cit.*, p. 6.

56. *Ibid.*

57. See the remarks of Lucien Rolland, president of Rolland Inc. (a Montreal-based competitor with Domtar), quoted in Wendie Kerr, "Caisse role termed in spirit of free enterprise", *Globe and Mail*, October 26, 1982, p. B-15. Similar views were expressed by Sam Hughes, president of the Canadian Chamber of Commerce, and Fred Burbidge, president of CP, in their respective testimony before the Senate Standing Committee on Legal and Constitutional Affairs (December 2, 1982) which considered Bill S-31.

58. See Allan Tupper, *Bill S-31 and the Federalism of State Capitalism*, Discussion Paper 18 (Kingston: Institute of Intergovernmental Relations, 1983).

59. See the testimony of Fred Burbidge at, Senate, Standing Committee, *Proceedings*, December 2, 1982, p. 7.

60. This concern runs throughout Burbidge's testimony. See *ibid*, p. 5-27.

61. In 1981, Dominion Textile's president, Tom Bell, was quoted as saying, "We feel a government agency isn't the kind of representation that should be on our board." Quoted in David Olive, "Caisse Unpopulaire," *Canadian Business* (May 1982), p. 101. The Caisse held 11 per cent of the corporation's equity as compared to 8.5 per cent held by the next largest shareholder, the Sobey retailing interests of Nova Scotia. The Sobey interests were represented on Dominion Textile's board of directors.

62. At the time of the federal government's "decision" in 1980 to provide a $200 million loan guarantee to Chrysler Canada,

the minister responsible for negotiating the federal government's assistance to Chrysler, Herb Gray, stated both publicly and in negotiations wth Chrysler president, Lee Iacocca, that financial support for the distressed automaker ought to be in return for government representation on the corporation's board of directors. This demand, which was quixotic in view of the fact that the United States administration had agreed to a similar loan guarantee without any such condition, was rejected as inconceivable by Chrysler's president. Government representation on the corporation's board of directors was considered an illegitimate intrusion upon private sector decision-making prerogatives, a view that received general support in the business community.

63. On March 2, 1982, the president of the Caisse said in a public address that under certain circumstances public sector interests superseded those of the private sector. While not a terribly controversial observation by itself, that it was made by the head of the Caisse at a time when that agency was following a policy of increasing the proportion of its portfolio invested in equities, and given the questions raised by the Domtar takeover in regard to the relationship between the investment decisions of the Caisse and the economic policy of the PQ government, contributed to uneasiness in the private sector (not to mention the federal government) over the instrumental role of the Caisse.

64 Under the terms of this written agreement Desmarais' ownership share in CP cannot exceed 15 per cent, except in the event that another party acquires more than 10 per cent of the corporation's shares. Should this happen, Desmarais would be entitled to maintain a margin of 5 per cent over the second largest shareholder. In return for this undertaking Desmarais received a position on the executive committee of CP's board, as well as the right to nominate another member to the board.

65 E.E. Schattschneider, *The Semi-Sovereign People* (New York: Holt, Rinehart and Winston, 1960), Chapter 1.

66. On the intergovernmental conflict dimension of the debate over S-31, see Allan Tupper, *Bill S-31 and the Federalism of*

State Capitalism, Discussion Paper 18 (Kingston: Institute of Intergovernmental Relations, 1983).

67. Personal interview; February 21, 1984.

Chapter 4

1. John Langford, "Public Corporations in the 1980s", *Canadian Public Administration*, Vol. 25, No. 4 (Winter 1982), p. 635.

2. G. B. Doern and J. Brothers, "Telesat Canada", in Doern and A. Tupper, *Public Corporations and Public Policy in Canada* (Montreal: IRPP, 1981), p. 244.

3. This is confirmed from personal interviews with industry principals, and from Telesat's dismal record of commercial performance. Indeed, transfer payments under the Telecom membership agreement have represented a crucial contribution to Telesat's income since the recent collapse of several pay television networks that were customers of the satellite corporation.

4. Personal interview, December 12, 1983.

5. The substitution of satellite for terrestrial carriage effectively changes jurisdiction from provincial to federal.

6. These potential levers of control are listed at page 2, in Chapter 1.

7. One industry principal on Telesat's board said it would be unreasonable to expect his company to participate in a venture with which it competed commercially. Personal interview, December 9, 1983.

8. Using two rather different performance criteria, i.e., management's goal of commercial viability and the industry's goal of controlling competition between telecommunications technologies, Telesat's record is mixed. On the first count, transfer payments made under the Connecting Agreement between Telesat and other member companies of Telecom Canada have comprised an important part of the corporation's earnings ($1.8 million of operating

revenues of $51.25 million in 1981; $5.2 million of $59 million in 1982; and $28 million of operating revenues of $88.1 in 1983). Telesat principals admit that these industry payments have represented a vital supplement to the corporation's income, without which commercial viability would have been impossible. But of course the *quid pro quo* for the financial safety net and guaranteed market provided under the Telesat/Telecom Communications Agreement is the effective control which the Telecom group has over the competitive development of the satellite system. Thus, the industry's interest in controlling the development of a telecommunications technology which, in some markets, is a substitute for terrestrial carriage is satisfied by Telesat's performance.

9. On May 27, 1982, an exchange of letters took place between Senator Jack Austin, then minister of state for social development, and Anthony Hampson, president of the CDC, acknowledging the government's intention to sell its interest in the corporation and creating the Canada Development Investment Corporation to carry out the eventual divestiture. For this reason 1982 is considered to mark the effective end of a phase in the CDC's history, when it was, potentially at least, an instrument of public policy.

10. See Stephen Brooks, "The State as Entrepreneur: From CDC to CDIC", *Canadian Public Administration* 26:4 (Winter 1983), pp. 527-529.

11. The influence which the government expected to have on CDC decision-making was both poorly-defined and a subject of contention among state actors. In his statement to the House of Commons during second reading of the CDC legislation, the minister of finance observed:

> Initially, the government will be the sole shareholder and it will always be the largest single shareholder. Because of the significant role the corporation has been given by its purpose and objects, the government will want to show a continuing interest in it and it is expected that the government will always want to hold at least 10 per cent of the voting shares. Thus it will always be in a position to exercise the degree of influence on the overall policies of the

corporation which would be appropriate to its shareholding.

A similar expectation of influence was expressed by Benson's parliamentary secretary, Patrick Mahoney, when he remarked: "We hope and intend it (CDC) will be able to act in whatever foreign ownership policy the government decides" (*Globe and Mail*, November 29, 1971). But the mechanisms of influence were never specified, and in practice the state shareholder was satisfied with the role of silent partner until the investment crisis of 1980, and the subsequent confrontation over the CDC chairmanship and board representation in 1981.

12. Using neo-mercantalist criteria of effectiveness, i.e., export promotion and internationalization of production, Jeanne Laux argues that the CDC has been a successful instrument of economic policy. However, she identifies the paradox of the CDC's international trade success when she writes: "Yet the very success of the CDC created the basis for autonomous action by state enterprise managers and generated increasingly incompatible perceptions of interest on the part of the corporation and the government. Not only has the CDC engaged in activities abroad which, unknown to government, contradicted established policy in the interest of competitive success, but the government has proven unable to exercise direction over the corporation's investment strategy." See Jeanne Kirk Laux, "State-Owned Enterprises and Foreign Economic Policy – the Limits of Neo-Mercantalism in Canada," paper prepared for the annual meeting of the Canadian Political Science Association, Vancouver, B.C., June 6, 1983, p. 17.

13. These figures cannot be ascertained with greater precision because of the consolidated nature of the eliminations category in the CDC's records accessible to the public.

14. These investment priorities were first stated in the CDC's 1972 *Annual Report*.

15. This analysis draws upon the information compiled by Dr. R. F. Kelly, from a survey of shareholders which he carried out for the CDC in 1976.

16. The CDC's consolidated loss of $125.8 million in 1982 represented the first annual loss in the corporation's history. Polysar accounted for $38.6 million of that loss. In 1983 the CDC's loss was reduced to $45 million, and Polysar returned to profitability ($2.1 million).

17. In its annual report the Caisse does not identify its investments in Quebec-based corporations separately from its general listing of equity investments.

18. A rank-ordering of the 150 largest (by assets) Quebec-controlled corporations is published annually by *Finance*, and this provides the basis for the population of businesses considered here.

19. While the list of private sector investments published by the Caisse is extensive, it is not exhaustive. Included are all investments in shares and bonds with a market value exceeding $5 million, as well as corporations in which the Caisse holds more than 10 per cent of voting rights.

20. Fournier, *op. cit.*, pp. 29, 40.

21. Quoted in *ibid* , p. 31 (author's translation).

22. For a description and analysis of the circumstances surrounding this legislation see, Allan Tupper, *Bill S-31 and the Federalism of State Capitalism* (Kingston: Institute of Intergovernmental Relations, Queen's University, 1983).

23. Quebec, *Débats de l'assemblée legislative*, 9 juin, 1965, p. 3325.

24. See "Le Trust Général", *Finance* (27 fevrier, 1984); "The Power link to 'supermarket shopping' ", *Financial Post* (April 21, 1984); and "Paul Desmarais entre par la grande porte en créant le no 2 canadien", *Finance* (4 juin, 1984).

25. Personal interview with an official of the Caisse, February 2, 1984.

26. Amy Booth, "Caisse's role as investor ruffles some feathers", *Financial Post* (May 19, 1984).

27. Quebec, Débats de l'assemblée legislative, 9 juin, 1965, p. 3311 (author's translation).

28. See Pierre Lortie's testimony before the Senate committee considering *The Corporate Shareholding Limitation Act*: Canada, Senate Standing Committee on Legal and Constitutional Affairs, Proceedings, December 2 1982.

29. Comparative figures are provided in *Finance* (9 avril, 1984), p. 8; and in C. Forget, *op. cit.*, p. 110.

30. The corporations in this group include Alcan, Bell Canada Enterprises, Canadian Pacific, Imperial Oil, Moore Corporation, Northern Telecom, the Royal Bank, Seagram Company, the Toronto-Dominion Bank, and Hiram Walker Resources.

31. Comparative figures are provided in *Finance* (9 avril, 1984), p. 8.

Chapter 5

1. See Catherine Eckel and Aidan Vining, "Toward a Positive Theory of Joint Enterprise", in W. Stanbury and F. Thompson, eds., *Managing Public Enterprises* (New York: Praeger, 1982).

2. Chwee Huat Tan, "The Public Enterprise as a Development Strategy: The Case of Singapore", *Annals of Public and Co-operative Economy* (Jan./Mar., 1975), pp. 61-85.

3. See chapter three in Chalmers Johnson, *Japan's Public Policy Companies* (Washington, D.C.: American Enterprise Institute for Public Policy Research, 1978).

4. Suggestive insights are provided in Andrew Shonfield's classic study, *Modern Capitalism* (London: Oxford University Press, 1965). Shonfield attempts to understand contemporary forms of state intervention in the context of national traditions which pre-date modern capitalism.

5. That this generally supportive orientation did not necessarily extend to a loyalty toward the PQ, much less to agreement with all of the main policies of the PQ

government, was demonstrated by the almost unanimous opposition of the francophone bourgeoisie to the *independantiste* option in the 1979 Referendum.

6. Robert Couzin, "The Canada Development Corporation: A Comparative Appraisal", *McGill Law Journal* (1971), p. 429.

7. Canada, Senate Standing Committee on Legal and Constitutional Affairs, Proceedings, December 2, 1982, p. 31:7.

8. William Dimma, "The Canada Development Corporation", Ph.D. dissertation, Harvard University, p. 10 (chapter one), mimeo.

Members of the Institute

Institute Management

Rod Dobell	President
Peter Dobell	Vice-President and Secretary-Treasurer
Yvon Gasse	Director, Small & Medium-Sized Business Program
Barbara L. Hodgins	Director, Western Resources Program
John Langford	Director, Governability Research Program
Barry Lesser	Director, Information Society Studies Program
Shirley Seward	Director, Studies in Social Policy
Frank Stone	Director, International Economics Program
Parker Staples	Director, Financial Services
Donald Wilson	Director, Communications
Tom Kent	Editor, *Policy Options Politiques*

Fellows- and Scholars-in-Residence:

Edgar Gallant	Fellow-in-Residence
Tom Kent	Fellow-in-Residence
Eric Kierans	Fellow-in-Residence
Jean-Luc Pepin	Fellow-in-Residence
Gordon Robertson	Fellow-in-Residence
David Burgess	Scholar-in-Residence
Barry Cooper	Scholar-in-Residence

Publications Available – April 1987

Order Address

The Institute for Research on Public Policy
P.O. Box 3670 South
Halifax, Nova Scotia
B3J 3K6

Leroy O. Stone & Claude Marceau	*Canadian Population Trends and Public Policy Through the 1980s.* 1977 $4.00
Raymond Breton	*The Canadian Condition: A Guide to Research in Public Policy.* 1977 $2.95
J.W. Rowley & W.T. Stanbury (eds.)	*Competition Policy in Canada: Stage II, Bill C-13.* 1978 $12.95
C.F. Smart & W.T. Stanbury (eds.)	*Studies on Crisis Management.* 1978 $9.95
W.T. Stanbury (ed.)	*Studies on Regulation in Canada.* 1978 $9.95
Michael Hudson	*Canada in the New Monetary Order: Borrow? Devalue? Restructure!* 1978 $6.95
David K. Foot (ed.)	*Public Employment and Compensation in Canada: Myths and Realities.* 1978 $10.95
Raymond Breton & Gail Grant Akian	*Urban Institutions and People of Indian Ancestry: Suggestions for Research.* 1979 $3.00
Thomas H. Atkinson	*Trends in Life Satisfaction Among Canadians, 1968-1977.* 1979 $3.00

W.E. Cundiff & Mado Reid (eds.)	*Issues in Canadian/U.S. Transborder Computer Data Flows.* 1979 $6.50
Meyer W. Bucovetsky (ed.)	*Studies in Public Employment and Compensation in Canada.* 1979 $14.95
Richard French & André Béliveau	*The RCMP and the Management of National Security.* 1979 $6.95
G. Bruce Doern & Allan M. Maslove (eds.)	*The Public Evaluation of Government Spending.* 1979 $10.95
Leroy O. Stone & Michael J. MacLean	*Future Income Prospects for Canada's Senior Citizens.* 1979 $7.95
Richard M. Bird	*The Growth of Public Employment in Canada.* 1979 $12.95
Richard J. Schultz	*Federalism and the Regulatory Process.* 1979 $1.50
Richard J. Schultz	*Le fédéralisme et le processus de réglementation.* 1979 $1.50
Elliot J. Feldman & Neil Nevitte (eds.)	*The Future of North America: Canada, the United States, and Quebec Nationalism.* 1979 $7.95
David R. Protheroe	*Imports and Politics: Trade Decision Making in Canada, 1968-1979.* 1980 $8.95
G. Bruce Doern	*Government Intervention in the Canadian Nuclear Industry.* 1980 $8.95
G. Bruce Doern & Robert W. Morrison (eds.)	*Canadian Nuclear Policies.* 1980 $14.95
Allan M. Maslove & Gene Swimmer	*Wage Controls in Canada: 1975-78: A Study of Public Decision Making.* 1980 $11.95
T. Gregory Kane	*Consumers and the Regulators: Intervention in the Federal Regulatory Process.* 1980 $10.95
Réjean Lachapelle & Jacques Henripin	*La situation démolinguistique au Canada: évolution passée et prospective.* 1980 $24.95
Albert Breton & Anthony Scott	*The Design of Federations.* 1980 $6.95
A.R. Bailey & D.G. Hull	*The Way Out: A More Revenue-Dependent Public Sector and How It Might Revitalize the Process of Governing.* 1980 $6.95
David R. Harvey	*Christmas Turkey or Prairie Vulture? An Economic Analysis of the Crow's Nest Pass Grain Rates.* 1980 $10.95
Donald G. Cartwright	*Official Language Populations in Canada: Patterns and Contacts.* 1980 $4.95
Richard M. Bird	*Taxing Corporations.* 1980 $6.95

Leroy O. Stone & Susan Fletcher	*A Profile of Canada's Older Population.* 1980 $7.95
Peter N. Nemetz (ed.)	*Resource Policy: International Perspectives.* 1980 $18.95
Keith A.J. Hay (ed.)	*Canadian Perspectives on Economic Relations With Japan.* 1980 $18.95
Dhiru Patel	*Dealing With Interracial Conflict: Policy Alternatives.* 1980 $5.95
Raymond Breton & Gail Grant	*La langue de travail au Québec : synthèse de la recherche sur la rencontre de deux langues.* 1981 $10.95
David M. Cameron (ed.)	*Regionalism and Supranationalism: Challenges and Alternatives to the Nation-State in Canada and Europe.* 1981 $9.95
Heather Menzies	*Women and the Chip: Case Studies of the Effects of Information on Employment in Canada.* 1981 $8.95
H.V. Kroeker (ed.)	*Sovereign People or Sovereign Governments.* 1981 $12.95
Peter Aucoin (ed.)	*The Politics and Management of Restraint in Government.* 1981 $17.95
Nicole S. Morgan	*Nowhere to Go? Possible Consequences of the Demographic Imbalance in Decision-Making Groups of the Federal Public Service.* 1981 $8.95
Nicole S. Morgan	*Où aller? Les conséquences prévisibles des déséquilibres démographiques chez les groupes de décision de la fonction publique fédérale.* 1981 $8.95
Raymond Breton, Jeffrey G. Reitz & Victor F. Valentine	*Les frontières culturelles et la cohésion du Canada.* 1981 $18.95
Peter N. Nemetz (ed.)	*Energy Crisis: Policy Response.* 1981 $10.95
James Gillies	*Where Business Fails.* 1981 $9.95
Allan Tupper & G. Bruce Doern (eds.)	*Public Corporations and Public Policy in Canada.* 1981 $16.95
Réjean Lachapelle & Jacques Henripin	*The Demolinguistic Situation in Canada: Past Trends and Future Prospects.* 1982 $24.95
Irving Brecher	*Canada's Competition Policy Revisited: Some New Thoughts on an Old Story.* 1982 $3.00
Ian McAllister	*Regional Development and the European Community: A Canadian Perspective.* 1982 $13.95
Donald J. Daly	*Canada in an Uncertain World Economic Environment.* 1982 $3.00

W.T. Stanbury & Fred Thompson	*Regulatory Reform in Canada.* 1982 $7.95
Robert J. Buchan, C. Christopher Johnston, T. Gregory Kane, Barry Lesser, Richard J. Schultz & W.T. Stanbury	*Telecommunications Regulation and the Constitution.* 1982 $18.95
Rodney de C. Grey	*United States Trade Policy Legislation: A Canadian View.* 1982 $7.95
John Quinn & Philip Slayton (eds.)	*Non-Tariff Barriers After the Tokyo Round.* 1982 $17.95
Stanley M. Beck & Ivan Bernier (eds.)	*Canada and the New Constitution: The Unfinished Agenda.* 2 vols. 1983 $10.95 (set)
R. Brian Woodrow & Kenneth B. Woodside (eds.)	*The Introduction of Pay-TV in Canada: Issues and Implications.* 1983 $14.95
E.P. Weeks & L. Mazany	*The Future of the Atlantic Fisheries.* 1983 $5.00
Douglas D. Purvis (ed.), assisted by Frances Chambers	*The Canadian Balance of Payments: Perspectives and Policy Issues.* 1983 $24.95
Roy A. Matthews	*Canada and the "Little Dragons": An Analysis of Economic Developments in Hong Kong, Taiwan, and South Korea and the Challenge/ Opportunity They Present for Canadian Interests in the 1980s.* 1983 $11.95
Charles Pearson & Gerry Salembier	*Trade, Employment, and Adjustment.* 1983 $5.00
Steven Globerman	*Cultural Regulation in Canada.* 1983 $11.95
F.R. Flatters & R.G. Lipsey	*Common Ground for the Canadian Common Market.* 1983 $5.00
Frank Bunn, assisted by U. Domb, D. Huntley, H. Mills, H. Silverstein	*Oceans from Space: Towards the Management of Our Coastal Zones.* 1983 $5.00
C.D. Shearing & P.C. Stenning	*Private Security and Private Justice: The Challenge of the 80s.* 1983 $5.00
Jacob Finkelman & Shirley B. Goldenberg	*Collective Bargaining in the Public Service: The Federal Experience in Canada.* 2 vols. 1983 $29.95 (set)
Gail Grant	*The Concrete Reserve: Corporate Programs for Indians in the Urban Work Place.* 1983 $5.00
Owen Adams & Russell Wilkins	*Healthfulness of Life.* 1983 $8.00
Yoshi Tsurumi with Rebecca R. Tsurumi	*Sogoshosha: Engines of Export-Based Growth.* (Revised Edition). 1984 $10.95

Raymond Breton & Gail Grant (eds.)	*The Dynamics of Government Programs for Urban Indians in the Prairie Provinces.* 1984 $19.95
Frank Stone	*Canada, The GATT and the International Trade System.* 1984 $15.00
Pierre Sauvé	*Private Bank Lending and Developing-Country Debt.* 1984 $10.00
Mark Thompson & Gene Swimmer	*Conflict or Compromise: The Future of Public Sector Industrial Relations.* 1984 $15.00
Samuel Wex	*Instead of FIRA: Autonomy for Canadian Subsidiaries?* 1984 $8.00
R.J. Wonnacott	*Selected New Developments in International Trade Theory.* 1984 $7.00
R.J. Wonnacott	*Aggressive US Reciprocity Evaluated with a New Analytical Approach to Trade Conflicts.* 1984 $8.00
Richard W. Wright	*Japanese Business in Canada: The Elusive Alliance.* 1984 $12.00
Paul K. Gorecki & W.T. Stanbury	*The Objectives of Canadian Competition Policy, 1888-1983.* 1984 $15.00
Michael Hart	*Some Thoughts on Canada-United States Sectoral Free Trade.* 1985 $7.00
J. Peter Meekison Roy J. Romanow & William D. Moull	*Origins and Meaning of Section 92A: The 1982 Constitutional Amendment on Resources.* 1985 $10.00
Conference Papers	*Canada and International Trade. Volume One: Major Issues of Canadian Trade Policy. Volume Two: Canada and the Pacific Rim.* 1985 $25.00 (set)
A.E. Safarian	*Foreign Direct Investment: A Survey of Canadian Research.* 1985 $8.00
Joseph R. D'Cruz & James D. Fleck	*Canada Can Compete! Strategic Management of the Canadian Industrial Portfolio.* 1985 $18.00
Barry Lesser & Louis Vagianos	*Computer Communications and the Mass Market in Canada.* 1985 $10.00
W.R. Hines	*Trade Policy Making in Canada: Are We Doing it Right?* 1985 $10.00
Bertrand Nadeau	*Britain's Entry into the European Economic Community and its Effect on Canada's Agricultural Exports.* 1985 $10.00
Paul B. Huber	*Promoting Timber Cropping: Policies Toward Non-Industrial Forest Owners in New Brunswick.* 1985 $10.00

Gordon Robertson	*Northern Provinces: A Mistaken Goal. 1985* $8.00
Petr Hanel	*La technologie et les exportations canadiennes du matériel pour la filière bois-papier.* 1985 $20.00
Russel M. Wills, Steven Globerman & Peter J. Booth	*Software Policies for Growth and Export.* 1986 $15.00
Marc Malone	*Une place pour le Québec au Canada.* 1986 $20.00
A. R. Dobell & S. H. Mansbridge	*The Social Policy Process in Canada.* 1986 $8.00
William D. Shipman (ed.)	*Trade and Investment Across the Northeast Boundary: Quebec, the Atlantic Provinces, and New England.* 1986 $20.00
Nicole Morgan	*Implosion: An Analysis of the Growth of the Federal Public Service in Canada (1945-1985).* 1986 $20.00
Nicole Morgan	*Implosion: analyse de la croissance de la Fonction publique fédérale canadienne (1945-1985).* 1986 $20.00
William A.W. Neilson & Chad Gaffield (eds.)	*Universities in Crisis: A Mediaeval Institution in the Twenty-first Century.* 1986 $20.00
Fred Wien	*Rebuilding the Economic Base of Indian Communities: The Micmac in Nova Scotia.* 1986 $20.00
D.M. Daly & D.C. MacCharles	*Canadian Manufactured Exports: Constraints and Opportunities.* 1986 $20.00
Gerald d'Amboise, Yvon Gasse & Rob Dainow	*The Smaller, Independent Manufacturer: 12 Quebec Case Studies.* 1986 $20.00
David J. Roy & Maurice A.M. de Wachter	*The Life Technologies and Public Policy.* 1986 $20.00
David Feeny, Gordon Guyatt & Peter Tugwell (eds.)	*Health Care Technology: Effectiveness, Efficiency, and Public Policy.* 1986 $20.00
International Symposium	*Les répercussions de l'informatisation en milieu de travail / The Impact of New Information Technologies on the Workplace.* 1986 $20.00
N.G. Papadopoulos	*Canada and the European Community: An Uncomfortable Partnership?* 1986 $15.00
W.T. Stanbury (ed.)	*Telecommunications Policy and Regulation: The Impact of Competition and Technological Change.* 1986 $22.00

James Gillies	*Facing Reality: Consultation, Consensus and Making Economic Policy for the 21st Century.* 1986 $15.95
International Seminar	*The Management of Water Resources – Proceedings / La gestion des ressources en eau – Actes.* 1986 $20.00
William J. Coffey & Mario Polèse (eds.)	*Still Living Together: Recent Trends and Future Directions in Canadian Regional Development.* 1987 $25.00
Bryan Schwartz	*First Principles, Second Thoughts: Aboriginal Peoples, Constitutional Reform and Canadian Statecraft.* 1987 $25.00
G.E. Salembier, Andrew R. Moroz and Frank Stone	*The Canadian Import File: Trade, Protection and Adjustment.* 1987 $20.00
Emer Killean	*Equality in the Economy: A Synthesis of the Proceedings of a Workshop / L'égalitarisme et l'économie : synthèse des débats d'atelier.* 1987 $10.00
Barry Lesser & Pamela Hall	*Telecommunications Services and Regional Development: The Case of Atlantic Canada.* 1987 $20.00
Stephen Brooks	*Who's in Charge? The Mixed Ownership Corporation in Canada.* 1987 $20.00